TROUT ON STRATEGY

TROUT ON STRATEGY

CAPTURING MINDSHARE, CONQUERING MARKETS

JACK TROUT

McGraw-Hill

New York   Chicago   San Francisco   Lisbon   London
Madrid   Mexico City   Milan   New Delhi   San Juan
Seoul   Singapore   Sydney   Toronto

6 7 8 9 0   DOC/DOC   0 9 8 7 6 5 4

ISBN 0-07-143794-0

McGraw-Hill books are available at special quantity discounts to use as premiums and sales promotions, or for use in corporate training programs. For more information, please write to the Director of Special Sales, Professional Publishing, McGraw-Hill, Two Penn Plaza, New York, NY 10121-2298. Or contact your local bookstore.

This book is printed on recycled, acid-free paper containing a minimum of 50% recycled, de-inked fiber.

Library of Congress Cataloging-in-Publication Data

Trout, Jack.
      Jack Trout on strategy : capturing mindshare, conquering markets / by Jack Trout.
            p.   cm.
      ISBN 0-07-143794-0 (alk. paper)
      1. Marketing—Management.   2. Strategic planning.   3. Success in business.   I. Title: Strategy.   II. Title.
      HF5415.13.T7353   2004
      658.4'012—dc22

                                                            2003027640

To my wife, who had
to live with me while I wrote
all my books

CONTENTS

PREFACE

It's been a long journey.

Starting at General Electric and winding through hundreds of companies in the United States and all over the globe, I've had the rare opportunity to understand what makes up success or failure in business.

These observations have been carefully catalogued and presented in 10 books and endless lectures to thousands of business people in every corner of the world.

What I've learned over and over again is that success isn't about having the right people, the right attitude, the right tools, the right role models, or the right organization. They all help, but they don't put you over the top.

It's all about having the right *strategy*.

That's because strategy sets the competitive direction, strategy dictates product planning, strategy tells you how to communicate internally and externally, strategy tells you on what to focus.

That's why it is so important to understand what strategy is all about. The better you understand strategy, the better you'll be able to select the right strategy for success. And, conversely, the better you'll be able to avoid the big trouble it's easy to encounter in our era of killer competition.

There has been no shortage of advice on this subject. In the past 30 years there have been 21,955 books written about strategic planning and marketing. One author will talk about sustainable competitive advantage. Another will announce that this idea is on its way out. One author talks about the importance of case studies. Another says that case studies shouldn't decide your strategy. And of course there is no end to jargon, such as *dynamic advantage, conjoint analysis, competitive dynamics, coevolution,* and my favorite, *sustainable competitive disadvantage.* All of this generates nothing but confusion.

But what makes things far worse is the fact that there are those who would say that strategy is one thing and marketing is another. But the truth is that they must be combined if you are to be successful. Marketing is what drives a business. And a great business strategy without proper marketing will often fail in a highly competitive world. To better understand this, consider the following example:

> *A small software company has come up with a better way to conduct project management. It*

uses a different methodology that deals with the uncertainties that surround most projects. One could say this company has a competitive advantage strategy with a superior product. All management has to do is hand the product to the marketing department staff and instruct them to tell the world about this wonderful software and why it is better. This approach would fail.

The problem is that this company has two very large, established competitors, as well as a number of smaller ones. They will quickly attack this smaller company and attempt to exclude it from the game. Their strategy will be to make their customers nervous about turning their project management over to an unknown. To get into the game, this company must come up with a marketing program that positions its new software as "The next generation of project management software." Everything the company does must drive this idea into the minds of its customers. It is establishing this "next generation" perception that will be the key to its success or failure. This will offset the natural concerns of dealing with an unknown. At the same time, no one wants to buy what is perceived to be an obsolete product.

As you can see by this example, the next-generation marketing of this improved software exploited a basic positioning principle that states that it is better to be first than to be better. The marketing is driving the business strategy. Thus my definition of *strategy*: What makes you unique and what is the best way to put that difference into the minds of your customers and prospects.

In this example, the new form of software that dealt with uncertainties was unique. The next-generation concept was the best way into the minds in the marketplace.

While I have written endlessly about success and failure, I've never focused on what the essence of good strategy is all about. So I went back and extracted from my many books the key guidelines to doing the right thing. Unlike my usual fare, there are a few examples but no detailed case histories in these extracts. There are mostly the important principles to follow.

It's a short course on what I've learned about strategy in my long journey through the business world.

Jack Trout

Strategy Is
All about Survival

Using good strategy is how you survive in a world of killer competition. Using good strategy is how you survive what I call *the tyranny of choice*.

In the beginning, choice was not a problem. When our earliest ancestors wondered "What's for dinner?" the answer wasn't very complicated. It was whatever animal in the neighborhood they could run down, kill, and drag back to the cave.

Today you walk into a cavernous supermarket and gaze out over a sea of different types and cuts of meats that someone else has run down, killed, dressed, and packaged for you.

Your problem is no longer catching dinner. Your problem is to try to figure out what to buy of the

1

hundreds of different packages staring back at you from the case. Red meat? White meat? The other white meat? Make-believe meat?

But that's only the beginning. Now you have to figure out what part of the animal you want. Loin? Chops? Ribs? Legs? Rump?

And what do you bring home for those family members who don't eat meat?

FISHING FOR DINNER

For that early ancestor, catching a fish was simply a matter of sharpening a stick and hoping to get lucky.

Today it can mean drifting into a Bass Pro Shop or an L.L. Bean or a Cabela's or an Orvis and being dazzled with a mind-boggling array of rods, reels, lures, clothing, boats, you name it.

At Bass Pro Shop's 300,000-square-foot flagship store in Springfield, Missouri, they will give you a haircut and then make a fishing lure out of the clippings for you.

Things have come a long way from that pointed stick.

GOING TO DINNER

Today many people figure it's better to have someone else figure out what's for dinner. But figuring out where to go is no easy decision in a place like New York City.

That's why, in 1979, Nina and Tim Zagat created the first New York restaurant survey to help us answer that difficult question of choice.

Today the pocket-sized *Zagat Survey* guides have become bestsellers, with 100,000 participants rating and reviewing restaurants in more than 40 major U.S. and foreign cities.

AN EXPLOSION OF CHOICE

What has changed in business over recent decades is the amazing proliferation of product choices in just about every category. It's been estimated that there are 1 million stock keeping units (SKUs) out there in America. An average supermarket has 40,000 SKUs. Now for the stunner—an average family gets 80 to 85 percent of its needs from 150 SKUs. That means there's a good chance you'll ignore 39,850 items in that store.

Buying a car in the 1950s meant the choice of a model from GM, Ford, Chrysler, or American Motors. Today you have your pick of cars, from GM, Ford, DaimlerChrysler, Toyota, Honda, Volkswagen, Fiat, Nissan, Mitsubishi, Renault, Suzuki, Daihatsu, BMW, Hyundai, Daiwa, Mazda, Isuzu, Kia, and Volvo. There were 140 motor vehicle models available in the early 1970s. There are 260 today.

Even in as thin a market as $175,000 Ferrari-type sports cars, there is a growing competition. You have Lamborghini, a new Bentley sports car, Aston Martin, and a new Mercedes called the Vision SLR.

Three decades ago, most manufacturers offered half a dozen vehicle styles. Today, there are so many (sport utility vehicles [SUVs], roadsters, hatchbacks, coupes, minivans, wagons, pickups, and "crossovers") that companies are being forced to outsource manufacturing. A manufacturer in Austria now makes BMWs, Jeeps, Mercedeses, and Saabs. Good old Henry Ford is probably looking down on this with some amusement. His concept was "all black and all the same."

And the proliferation in the choice of tires for these cars is even worse. It used to be Goodyear, Firestone, General, and Sears. Today you have the likes of Goodyear, Bridgestone, Cordovan, Michelin, Cooper, Dayton, Firestone, Kelly, Dunlop, Sears, Multi-Mile, Pirelli, General, Armstrong, Sentry, Uniroyal, and 22 other brands.

The big difference is that what used to be national markets with local companies competing for business has become a global market with everyone competing for everyone's business everywhere.

CHOICE IN HEALTH CARE

Consider something as basic as health care. In the old days you had your doctor, your hospital, Blue Cross, and perhaps Aetna/US Healthcare, Medicare, or Medicaid. Now you have to deal with new names such as MedPartners, Cigna, Prucare, Columbia, Kaiser, Wellpoint, Quorum, Oxford, Americare, and Multiplan, and concepts like health maintenance organizations (HMOs), peer review organizations (PROs), physician hospital organizations (PHOs), and preferred provider organizations (PPOs).

CHOICE IS SPREADING

What we just described is what has happened to the U.S. market, which, of the world's markets, has by far the most choice (because our citizens have the most money and the most marketing people trying to get it from them).

Consider an emerging nation such as China. After decades of buying generic food products manufactured by state-owned enterprises, China's consumers now can choose from a growing array of domestic and foreign brand-name products each time they go shopping. According to a recent survey, a national market for brand-name food products has already begun to emerge. Already China has 135 national food brands from which to pick. They've got a long way to go, but they are on their way to some serious tyranny.

Some markets are far from emerging. Countries such as Liberia, Somalia, North Korea, and Tanzania are so poor and chaotic that choice is but a gleam in people's eyes.

THE LAW OF DIVISION

What drives choice is the *law of division*, which was first published in the 1993 book I wrote with Al Ries, *The 22 Immutable Laws of Marketing*.

Like the computer, the automobile started off as a single category. Three brands (Chevrolet, Ford, and Plymouth) dominated the market. Then the category divided.

Today a wired household has over 150 channels from which to choose. And they are threatening us with "streaming video" that promises to make the cable industry's dream of a 500-channel universe look pathetically unambitious. With all that, if you flip through the channels and try to find something to watch, by the time you find it the show will be over.

Division is a process that is unstoppable. If you have any doubts, consider the accompanying table on the explosion of choice.

THE "CHOICE INDUSTRY"

All this has led to an entire industry dedicated to helping people with their choices. We've already talked about Zagat's restaurant guides.

The Explosion of Choice

Item	Early 1970s	Late 1990s
Vehicle models	140	260
KFC menu items	7	14
Vehicle styles	654	1,121
Frito-Lay chip varieties	10	78
SUV styles	8	38
Breakfast cereals	160	340
PC models	0	400
Pop-Tart varieties	3	29
Software titles	0	250,000
Soft drink brands	20	87
Web sites	0	4,757,894
Bottled water brands	16	50
Movie releases	267	458
Milk types	4	19
Airports	11,261	18,202
Colgate toothpaste varieties	2	17
Magazine titles	339	790
Mouthwashes	15	66
New book titles	40,530	77,446
Dental flosses	12	64
Community colleges	886	1,742
Prescription drugs	6,131	7,563
Amusement parks	362	1,174
Over-the-counter pain relievers	17	141
TV screen sizes	5	15
Levi's jean styles	41	70
Houston TV channels	5	185
Running shoe styles	5	285
Radio stations	7,038	12,458
Women's hosiery styles	5	90
McDonald's menu items	13	43
Contact lens types	1	36

Everywhere you turn, someone is offering advice on things like which of the 8000 mutual funds to buy. Or how to find the right dentist in St. Louis. Or the right MBA program from among hundreds of business schools. (Will it help you get a Wall Street job?)

Magazines like *Consumer Reports* and *Consumers Digest* deal with the onslaught of products and choices by rotating the categories on which they report. The only problem is that they go into so much detail that you're more confused than when you started.

Consumer psychologists say this sea of choices is driving us bonkers. Consider what Carol Moog has to say on the subject: "Too many choices, all of which can be fulfilled instantly, indulged immediately, keeps children—and adults—infantile. From a marketing perspective, people stop caring, get as fat and fatigued as foie gras geese, and lose their decision-making capabilities. They withdraw and protect against the overstimulation; they get 'bored.'"

CHOICE CAN BE CRUEL

The dictionary defines *tyranny* as absolute power that often is harsh or cruel.

So it is with choice. With the enormous competition, markets today are driven by choice. The customer has so many good alternatives that you pay dearly for your mistakes. Your competitors get your business and you don't get it back very easily. Companies that don't understand this will not survive. (Now *that's* cruel.)

Just look at some of the names on the headstones in the brand graveyard: American Motors, Burger Chef, Carte Blanche, Eastern Airlines, Gainesburgers, Gimbel's, Hathaway shirts, Horn & Hardart, Mr. Salty Pretzels, Philco, Trump Shuttle, VisiCalc, Woolworth's.

And this is only a short list of names that are no longer with us.

AND IT WILL ONLY GET WORSE

Don't bet that all this will calm down. I feel that it will get worse for the simple reason that choice appears to beget more choice.

In a book titled *Faster*, author James Glieck outlines what can only be called a bewildering future, which he describes as "The acceleration of just about everything." Consider the following scenario:

> *This proliferation of choice represents yet another positive feedback loop—a whole menagerie of such loops. The more information glut bears*

down on you, the more Internet "portals" and search engines and infobots arise to help by pouring information your way. The more telephone lines you have, the more you need. The more patents, the more patent lawyers and patent search services. The more cookbooks you buy or browse, the more you feel the need to serve your guests something new; the more cookbooks you need. The complications beget choice; the choices inspire technology; the technologies create complication. Without the distribution and manufacturing efficiencies of the modern age, without toll-free numbers and express delivery and bar codes and scanners and, above all, computer, the choices would not be multiplying like this.

Ladies and gentlemen, we haven't seen anything yet.

WHAT REALLY WORKS

Nitkin Nohria, William Joyce, and Bruce Roberson conducted what was described in the *Harvard Business Review* (July 2003) as "the most rigorous study of management practices ever undertaken." They reported that what really works is not CRM, TQM, BPR, and other tools or fads. Superior performance in this competitive world is all about mastering business basics. Vince

Lombardi of Green Bay Packers fame would have described it as good blocking and tackling.

Their number-one basic was "Devising and maintaining a clearly stated, focused strategy." To achieve excellence in strategy is to be clear about what the strategy is and to constantly communicate it to customers, employees, and shareholders. It's a simple, focused value proposition. In other words, what's the reason to buy from you instead of one of your competitors?

THE DEFINITION OF STRATEGY

If using good strategy is how you are to survive, a good starting point is to look at the definition of strategy, as found in *Webster's New World Dictionary:*

> *The science of planning and directing large-scale military operations. Of maneuvering forces into the most advantageous position prior to actual engagement with the enemy.*

You'll notice that this is a military word with the enemy in mind. If you are going to seek that "most advantageous position," you must first study, understand, and maneuver around the battleground. And that battleground is in the minds of your customers and prospects.

SUMMATION
....

In a tough world,
using strategy
is how you survive.

Strategy Is
All about Perceptions

Positioning is how you differentiate yourself in the mind of your prospect. It's also a body of work on how the mind works in the process of communication.

The first words on this important subject go back to 1969, when I wrote an article in *Industrial Marketing Management* titled "Positioning Is a Game People Play in Today's Me-Too Marketplace." (That's when choice first began to rear its ugly head.)

Here's an untold secret. I chose the word *positioning* because of the dictionary definition of strategy offered in the previous chapter: Finding the most advantageous position against the enemy.

Then, in 1981, my ex-partner Al Ries and I published the very popular *Positioning: The Battle for Your Mind*. In 1996, I wrote *The New Positioning: The Latest on the World's #1 Business Strategy*. This latter book made the simple case that your business strategy will succeed or fail depending on how well you understand the five most important elements in the positioning process. Here's a short course on each of these elements.

1. MINDS ARE LIMITED

Like the memory bank of a computer, the mind has a slot or position for each bit of information it has chosen to retain. In operation, the mind is a lot like a computer.

But there is one important difference. A computer has to accept what you put into it. The mind does not. In fact, it's quite the opposite. The mind rejects new information that doesn't compute. It accepts only new information that matches its current state of mind.

AN INADEQUATE CONTAINER

Not only does the human mind reject information that does not match its prior knowledge or experience, it doesn't have much prior knowledge or experience to work with.

In our overcommunicated society, the human mind is a totally inadequate container.

According to Harvard psychologist George A. Miller, the average human mind cannot deal with more than seven units at a time, which is why seven is a popular number for lists that have to be remembered. Seven-digit phone numbers, the Seven Wonders of the World, seven-card stud, Snow White and the Seven Dwarfs.

Ask someone to name all the brands he or she remembers in a given product category. Rarely will anyone name more than seven. And that's for a high-interest category. For low-interest products, the average consumer can usually name no more than one or two brands.

Try listing all ten of the Ten Commandments. If that's too difficult, how about the seven danger signals of cancer? Or the Four Horsemen of the Apocalypse?

If our mental storage bowl is too small to handle questions like these, how in the world are we going to keep track of all those brand names that have been multiplying like rabbits over the years?

THE PRODUCT LADDER

To cope with the product explosion, people have learned to rank products and brands in the mind. Perhaps this can best be visualized by imagining a series of ladders in the mind. On each step is a brand name. And each different ladder represents a different product category.

15

Some ladders have many steps. (Seven is many.) Others have few, if any.

A competitor that wants to increase its share of the business must either dislodge the brand above (a task that is usually impossible) or somehow relate its brand to the other company's position.

Yet too many companies embark on marketing and advertising programs as if the competitor's position did not exist. They advertise their products in a vacuum and are disappointed when their messages fail to get through.

Moving up the ladder in the mind can be extremely difficult if the brands above have a strong foothold and no leverage or positioning strategy is applied.

An advertiser who wants to introduce a new product category must carry in a new ladder. This, too, is difficult, especially if the new category is not positioned against the old one. The mind has no room for what's new and different unless it's related to the old.

That's why if you have a truly new product, it's often better to tell the prospect what the product is not, rather than what it is.

The first automobile, for example, was called a *horseless carriage*, a name that allowed the public to position the concept against the existing mode of transportation.

Phrases like *off-track betting*, *lead-free gasoline*, and *sugar-free soda* are all examples of how new concepts can best be positioned against the old.

THE NEWS FACTOR

One other way of overcoming the mind's natural stinginess when it comes to accepting new information is to work hard at presenting your message as important *news*.

Too many advertisers try to entertain or be clever. In so doing, they often overlook the news factor in their story.

The Roper Starch research people can demonstrate that headlines which contain news score better in readership than those that don't. Unfortunately, most creative people see this kind of thinking as *old* news.

If people think you've got an important message to convey, generally they'll open their eyes or ears long enough to absorb what you've got to say.

---

2. MINDS HATE CONFUSION

Human beings rely more heavily on learning than any other species that has ever existed.

"Learning is the way animals and human beings acquire new information," says a scientist at Columbia University's Center for Neurobiology and Behavior. "Memory is the way they retain that information over time."

"Memory is not just your ability to remember a phone number," says experimental psychologist Lynne

17

Reder, who studied memory at Carnegie Mellon University. "Rather, it's a dynamic system that's used in every other facet of thought processing. We use memory to see. We use it to understand language. We use it to find our way around."

So if memory is so important, what's the secret of being remembered?

KEEP IT SIMPLE

When asked what single event was most helpful to him in developing the theory of relativity, Albert Einstein is reported to have answered: "Figuring out how to think about the problem."

John Sculley, former chairman of Apple computer, put it this way:

> *Everything we have learned in the industrial age has tended to create more and more complication. I think that more and more people are learning that you have to simplify, not complicate. That is a very Asian idea—that simplicity is the ultimate sophistication.*

Professional communicators, such as the network broadcasters, understand this principle very well. They keep their word selection very simple. (More on this in Chapter 6.)

THE PROBLEM OF COMPLEXITY

We tend to think of boredom as arising from a lack of stimuli. A sort of information *under*load.

But more and more commonly, boredom is arising from excessive stimulation or information overload.

Information, like energy, tends to degrade into entropy—into just noise, redundancy, and banality. To put it another way, the fast horse of information outruns the slow horse of meaning.

Complicated answers don't help anybody. For instance, every executive wants information, because the difference between a decision and a guess often comes down to information. But today's executives don't want to be buried alive in printouts and reports.

PRODUCTS WITH MORE

We have this terrific word for new products: *more*.

Marketing people love to talk about *convergence*, the process whereby technologies are merged and wondrous new products are introduced with more and more features. Here's an early list of casualties:

- AT&T's EO Personal Communicator, a cellular phone, fax, electronic mail device, personal organizer, and pen-based computer

- Okidata's Doc-it, a desktop printer, fax, scanner, and copier

- Apple's Newton, a fax, beeper, calendar-keeper, and pen-based computer
- Sony's multimedia player, with display screen and interactive keyboard

But those are simple compared to Bill Gates's version of the wallet of the future. He sees it as a device that will combine or replace keys, charge cards, personal identification, cash, writing implements, a passport, and pictures of the kids. It also would have a global positioning system so you can always tell where you are.

Will any of these products make it?

Not likely. They are too confusing and too complex. Most of the people in the world still can't figure out how to record on their VCRs.

People resist that which is confusing, and cherish that which is simple. They want to push a button and watch it work.

CONFUSING CONCEPTS

The basic concepts behind some products predict failure. Not because they don't work but because they don't make sense.

Consider Mennen's Vitamin E deodorant. That's right, you sprayed a vitamin under your arm.

Present this concept to a group of consumers, and, guaranteed, you'll get a laugh. It doesn't make sense unless you want the healthiest, best-fed armpits in the nation. No one is going to try to figure *that* one out.

It quickly failed.

Consider Extra-Strength Maalox Whip Antacid. That's right, you sprayed a glob of cream whip on a spoon and took it for your heartburn.

This had a hard time even getting on the shelves, as the druggists laughed the salespeople out of the store. Antacids are tablets or liquids, not whipped cream.

At the time all it did was give the manufacturer, William H. Rorer, a costly case of indigestion.

Confusion strikes again.

---

3. MINDS ARE INSECURE

Aristotle would have been a lousy ad man. Pure logic is no guarantee of a winning argument.

Minds tend to be emotional, not rational.

Why do people buy what they buy? Why do people act the way they do in the marketplace? According to psychologists Robert Settle and Pamela Alreck, in their book *Why They Buy*, customers don't know, or they won't say.

When you ask people why they made a particular purchase, the responses they give are often not very accurate or useful.

That may mean they really do know, but they're reluctant to tell you the right reason.

More often, they really *don't* know precisely what their own motives are.

Even when it comes to recall, minds are insecure and tend to remember things that no longer exist. Recognition of a well-established brand often stays high over a long time period, even if advertising support is dropped.

BUYING WHAT OTHERS BUY

My experience is that people don't know what they want. (So why ask them?)

More times than not, people buy what they think they should have. They're sort of like sheep, following the herd.

Do most people really need a four-wheel-drive vehicle? (No.) If they did need them, why didn't they become popular years ago? (Not fashionable.)

The main reason for this kind of behavior is insecurity, a subject about which many scientists have written extensively.

FIVE FORMS OF PERCEIVED RISK

Minds are insecure for many reasons. One reason is perceived risk in doing something as basic as making a purchase.

Behavioral scientists say there are five forms of perceived risk:

1. *Monetary risk.*   There's a chance I could lose my money on this.
2. *Functional risk.*   Maybe it won't work, or do what it's supposed to do.
3. *Physical risk.*   It looks a little dangerous. I could get hurt.
4. *Social risk.*   I wonder what my friends will think if I buy this?
5. *Psychological risk.*   I might feel guilty or irresponsible if I buy this.

FOLLOWING THE HERD

One of the most interesting pieces of work on why people follow the herd was written by Robert Cialdini. He talks of the principle of *social proof* as a potent weapon of influence:

> *This principle states that we determine what is correct by finding out what other people think is correct. The principle applies especially to the way we decide what constitutes correct behavior. We view a behavior as correct in a given situation to the degree that we see others performing it.*

The tendency to see an action as appropriate when others are doing it works quite well normally. As a rule, we will make fewer mistakes by acting in accord with social evidence than by acting contrary to it. Usually, when a lot of people are doing something, it is the right thing to do.

This feature of the principle of social proof is simultaneously its major strength and its major weakness. Like the other weapons of influence, it provides a convenient shortcut for determining the way to behave but, at the same time, makes one who uses the shortcut vulnerable to the attacks of profiteers who lie in wait along its path.

THE TESTIMONIAL

When people are uncertain, they often will look to others to help them decide how to act.

That's why one of the oldest devices known to advertising is the *testimonial*.

A testimonial attacks the insecure mind on several emotional fronts—a trifecta of vanity, jealousy, and fear of being left out.

Stanley Resor, one-time head of J. Walter Thompson, called it "the spirit of emulation." Said Resor, "We want to copy those whom we deem superior in taste or knowledge or experience."

Today's favorite testimonials involve the athletes. Michael Jordan and Tiger Woods are the best of the breed.

THE BANDWAGON

Creating a *bandwagon effect* is another powerful technique for dealing with the insecure mind.

Originally, a bandwagon was an elaborately decorated wagon used to transport musicians in a parade. Today it has come to mean any cause or trend that takes an increasing number of people along for the ride.

Polls and panels always make good authority figures to create the bandwagon. (J.D. Powers surveys are a good example.)

Another bandwagon strategy for dealing with the insecure mind is that of the "fastest-growing" or "largest-selling." It says that others obviously think we have a pretty good product.

THE HERITAGE

Marketers also display their tradition and culture as a way of getting you on their bandwagon. (After all, how can a mere consumer argue with heritage?)

As early as 1919, a Steinway piano was being described in an advertisement as "the instrument of the immortals."

Cross trumpets its pens and mechanical pencils as "flawless classics, since 1846."

Glenlivet positions itself as "the father of all Scotch. His Majesty's Government bestowed on The Glenlivet Distillery the very first license under The Act of 1823 to distill single malt whisky in the Highlands."

Coke has exploited its heritage in inventing the cola by calling itself "the real thing." That is the company's most powerful strategy.

4. MINDS DON'T CHANGE

There has always been a general feeling in the marketing industry that new-product advertising should generate higher interest than advertising for established brands.

But it turns out that we're actually more impressed by what we already know (or buy) than by what's "new."

One research organization, McCollum Spielman, has tested more than 22,000 TV commercials over 23 years. Almost 6000 of those commercials were for new products in 10 product categories.

What did they learn? Greater persuasion ability and attitude shifts—the so-called new-product excitement— were evident in only 1 of the 10 categories (pet products) when comparing new brands to established brands.

In the other 9 categories—ranging from drugs to beverages to personal hygiene items—there was no real difference, no burst of excitement, enabling consumers to distinguish between established brands and new brands.

With thousands of different commercials across hundreds of different brands, you can pretty much rule out "creativity" as the difference in persuasion. It comes back to what we're familiar with, what we're already comfortable with.

TRYING TO CHANGE ATTITUDES

In the book *The Reengineering Revolution*, MIT professor-turned-consultant Michael Hammer calls human beings' innate resistance to change "the most perplexing, annoying, distressing, and confusing part" of reengineering.

To help us better understand this resistance, a book titled *Attitudes and Persuasion* offers some insights. Written by Richard Petty and John Cacioppo, it spends some time on "belief systems." Here's their take on why minds are so hard to change:

> *The nature and structure of belief systems is important from the perspective of an informational theorist, because beliefs are thought to provide the cognitive foundation of an attitude.*
>
> *In order to change an attitude, then, it is presumably necessary to modify the information on which that attitude rests. It is generally*

necessary, therefore, to change a person's beliefs, eliminate old beliefs, or introduce new beliefs.

And you're going to do all that with a 30-second commercial?

WHAT PSYCHOLOGISTS SAY

The Handbook of Social Psychology reinforces how tough it is to change attitudes:

Any program to change attitudes offers formidable problems. The difficulty of changing a person's basic beliefs, even through so elaborate and intense a procedure as psychotherapy, becomes understandable, as does the fact that procedures that are effective in changing some attitudes have little effect on others.

And what makes things even worse is that truth has no real bearing on these issues. Check out this observation:

People have attitudes on a staggeringly wide range of issues. They seem to know what they like (and especially dislike) even regarding objects about which they know little, such as Turks, or which have little relevance to their daily concerns, like life in outer space.

28

So, to paraphrase an old TV show, if your assignment, Mr. Phelps, is to change people's minds, don't accept the assignment.

---

5. MINDS CAN LOSE FOCUS

In days gone by, most big brands were clearly perceived by their customers. The mind, like a camera, had a very clear picture of what its favorite brands were all about.

When Anheuser-Busch proudly proclaimed that "This Bud's for you," the customer knew exactly what was being served.

The same went for Miller High Life, or plain old Coors beer.

But in the past decade, Budweiser flooded the market with a vast variety of regular, light, draft, clear, cold-brewed, dry-brewed, and ice-brewed beers.

Now the statement "This Bud's for you" can only elicit the question, "Which one do you have in mind?"

That clear perception in the mind is now badly out of focus. It's no wonder the King of Beers is starting to lose its following.

THE LINE EXTENSION TRAP

Loss of focus is really all about *line extension*. And no issue in marketing is so controversial.

In our 1972 *Advertising Age* articles, Al Ries and I cautioned companies not to fall into what we called "the line extension trap."

Positioning: The Battle for Your Mind contains two chapters on the problem of line extension.

In *The 22 Immutable Laws of Marketing*, it became the single most violated law.

Not that our lack of approval has slowed anyone down. In fact, quite the opposite has been true. "Extending brand equity" has become all the rage, as companies like Coca-Cola talk about concepts such as "megabrands."

For years we were the lonely voices railing against line extension. Even the *Journal of Consumer Marketing* noticed this: "Ries and Trout stand alone as the only outright critics of the practice of brand extension." (Our minds don't change.)

That lasted until the *Harvard Business Review* (November–December 1994) rendered its verdict: "Unchecked product-line extension can weaken a brand's image, disturb trade relations, and disguise cost increases."

Keep it up, guys.

A MATTER OF PERSPECTIVE

The difference in views on this subject is essentially a matter of perspective. Companies look at their brands from an economic point of view. To gain cost efficiencies and trade acceptance, they are quite willing to turn a highly focused brand, one that stands for a certain type of product or idea, into an unfocused brand that represents two or three or more types of products or ideas.

I look at the issue of line extension from the point of view of the mind. The more variations you attach to the brand, the more the mind loses focus. Gradually, a brand like Chevrolet comes to mean nothing at all.

Scott, the leading brand of toilet tissue, line-extended its name into Scotties, Scottkins, ScotTowels. Pretty soon "Scott" flunked the shopping-list test. (You can't write down "Scott" and have it mean anything.)

DANGER: A WELL-FOCUSED SPECIALIST

Things would have been fine in the land of Scott if the likes of Mr. Whipple and his squeezable Charmin tissue hadn't arrived on the scene. (The more you lose focus, the more vulnerable you become.) It didn't take long for Charmin to become the number-one tissue.

The course of business history seems to verify our concerns.

For years, Procter & Gamble's Crisco brand was the leading shortening. Then the world turned to vegetable oil. Of course, Procter & Gamble turned to Crisco Oil.

So who was the big winner in the corn-oil melee? That's right, Mazola.

Then Mazola noticed the success of a no-cholesterol corn-oil margarine. So Mazola introduced Mazola Corn Oil Margarine.

So who was the winner in the corn-oil-margarine category? You're right, it was Fleischmann's.

In each case, the specialist or the well-focused competitor was the winner.

THE SPECIALIST'S WEAPONS

Here are some thoughts on why the specialist brand appears to make such an impression on the mind. (More on this in Chapter 5.)

First, the specialist can focus on one product, one benefit, one message. This focus enables the marketer to put a sharp point on the message that quickly drives it into the mind. Some examples:

Domino's Pizza can focus on its home delivery. Pizza Hut has to talk about *both* home delivery and sitdown service.

Duracell can focus on long-lasting alkaline batteries. Eveready had to talk about flashlight, heavy-duty, rechargeable, and alkaline batteries. (Then Eveready got smart and went to the Energizer only, a good move on its part.)

Castrol can focus on its specialty oil for small, high-performance engines. Pennzoil and Quaker State are marketed for all types of engines.

Another weapon of the specialist is the ability to be perceived as the expert or the best. Intel is the best in microchips. Philadelphia is the best brand in cream cheese. (The original, so to speak.)

Finally, the specialist can become the generic for the category:

Xerox became the generic word for copying. ("Please xerox that for me.")

Federal Express became the generic word for overnight delivery. ("I'll FedEx it to you.")

3M's *Scotch tape* became the generic word for cellophane tape. ("I'll scotch-tape it together.")

Even though the lawyers hate it, making the brand name a generic is the ultimate weapon in the marketing wars. But it's something only a specialist can do. The generalist can't become a generic.

Nobody ever says, "Get me a beer from the GE."

SUMMATION
....

**Perception is reality.
Don't get confused by facts.**

Strategy Is All about Being Different

As you read in Chapter 2, in the land of positioning, a successful strategy is based on finding a way to be different from your sea of competitors. What is the reason to buy your brand instead of another?

While others have written about the importance of "differentiation," few if any have presented the many ways you can do it. This is why I cowrote the book *Differentiate or Die*. But before we get to the how-to-do-it strategies, it's important to focus on the how-not-to-do-it strategies. In other words, quality and customer orientation are rarely differentiation ideas.

THE WAR ON QUALITY

Yes, the 1990s witnessed a war on quality. Business leaders demanded tools and techniques to measure it. An army of gurus and academics marched forth with books and endless diatribes on how to define, predict, and ensure this elusive creature called quality.

On they came, a numbing maze of acronyms and buzzwords: the Seven Old Tools, the Seven New Tools, TQM, SPC, QFD, CQL, and just about any other combination of three letters you could string together.

In 1993 alone, there were 422 books in print with the word *quality* in the title. Today, there are half as many. (We must have won the war.)

Survey after survey today acknowledges that consumers see quality improvements all around them. Cars are better made. Small appliances last longer. Computers come with instruction manuals in simple English.

The editorial director at polling firm Roper Starch Worldwide explains it this way:

> *All brands have to work harder to get ahead today. They keep upping the ante to meet consumers' needs. The consumer is still king. And it doesn't look like the equation is going to change anytime soon. Consumers have not slacked off in their demands as the economy has improved. If anything, they've grown more demanding.*

It sounds as though quality only keeps you in the game.

THE WAR FOR CUSTOMER SATISFACTION

If quality were a war, then the assault on the customer would be Armageddon.

A landmark study published in *Harvard Business Review* argued that companies could improve profits by at least 25 percent by reducing customer defections by 5 percent. Whoa, Nellie. You could hear the alarm bells going off in boardrooms across the land.

Seminars, books, and counselors told us 1001 ways to dazzle, love, partner with, and just plain hang on to that person called a customer.

We were told the customer is a collaborator. The customer is the CEO. The customer is king. The customer is a butterfly. (Don't even ask.)

Customer feedback meant every complaint was a gift. Better aftermarketing would keep a customer for life. Learning how to manage in total customer time would solve all your problems.

It was enough to drive you into the not-for-profit world.

As the century rolled over, *Marketing Management* (Spring 1999) concluded, "Practically every company today is geared up to satisfy its customers. 'We do whatever it takes' is the everyday refrain."

Somewhere along the way, customer satisfaction has become a given, not a differentiator.

So, now that we've cleared that up, let's get on with the how-to strategies.

BEING FIRST IS A DIFFERENTIATING IDEA

Getting into the mind with a new idea or product or benefit gives you an enormous advantage. That's because, as described in Chapter 2, minds don't like change.

Psychologists refer to this as "keeping on." Many experiments have shown the magnetic attraction of the status quo. Most decision makers display a strong bias toward alternatives that perpetuate the current situation.

The bottom line: People tend to stick with what they've got. If you meet someone a little better than your wife or husband, it's really not worth making the switch, what with attorneys' fees and dividing up the house and kids.

And if you're there first, when your competitors try to copy you, all they will be doing is reinforcing your idea. It's much easier to get into the mind first than to try to convince someone you have a better product than the one that did get there first.

FIRSTS THAT ARE STILL FIRSTS

Harvard was the first college in America and it's still perceived as the leader.

Time magazine still is the leader over *Newsweek*. *People* leads over *Us*. *Playboy* leads over *Penthouse*. Chrysler, which introduced minivans, is still the leader in minivans. Hewlett-Packard leads in desktop laser printers, Sun in workstations, Xerox in copiers. The list goes on and on.

In the mind, the fact that they pioneered the category or product makes them different from their followers. They get a special status because they were the first to the top of the mountain.

This is why Evian, the French mineral water, is spending $20 million on advertising to remind consumers it is *l'original*.

ATTRIBUTE OWNERSHIP IS A WAY TO DIFFERENTIATE

Attribute is one of those marketing words that is used widely but not really understood. So let's get our definitions straight before we plunge on.

First, an attribute is a characteristic, peculiarity, or distinctive feature of a person or thing. Next, persons or things have a mixture of attributes. Each person is different in terms of sex, size, intelligence, skills, and attractiveness. Each product, depending on the category, also has a set of different attributes. Each toothpaste, for example, is different from other toothpastes in terms of cavity prevention, plaque prevention, taste, tooth whitening, and breath protection.

OWNING AN ATTRIBUTE

What makes a person or product unique is being known for one of these attributes. Marilyn Monroe was known for her attractiveness. Crest toothpaste is known for its cavity prevention. Marilyn might have had a high degree of intelligence, but it wasn't important. What made her special was that pinup beauty. The same with Crest, as it's all about fighting cavities. What it tastes like isn't important.

Attribute ownership is probably the number-one way to differentiate a product or service. But beware, you can't own the same attribute or position that your competitor owns. You must seek out another attribute.

Too often a company attempts to emulate the leader: "They must know what works," goes the rationale, "so let's do something similar." Not good thinking.

It's much better to search for an opposite attribute that will allow you to play off against the leader: The key word here is *opposite*—similar won't do.

Coca-Cola was the original and thus the choice of older people. Pepsi successfully positioned itself as the choice of the younger generation.

The world of bourbon is dominated by the two Js, Jim Beam and Jack Daniel's. So Maker's Mark set out to own an attribute that makes its smaller sales more attractive: "Handcrafting our bourbon to produce a smooth, soft taste."

Since Crest owned cavity prevention, other toothpastes avoided cavity prevention and jumped on other attributes, such as taste, whitening ability, breath protection, and more recently, inclusion of baking soda.

If you're not a leader, your word has to have a narrow focus. Even more important, however, your word has to be "available" in your category. No one else can have a lock on it.

LEADERSHIP IS A WAY TO DIFFERENTIATE

Leadership is the most powerful way to differentiate a brand. The reason is that it's the most direct way to establish the credentials of a brand. And credentials are the collateral you put up to guarantee the performance of your brand.

Also, when you have leadership credentials, your prospect is likely to believe almost anything you say about your brand (because you're the leader). Humans tend to equate "bigness" with success, status, and leadership. We give respect and admiration to the biggest.

OWNING A CATEGORY

Powerful leaders can take ownership of the word that stands for the category. You can test the validity of a leadership claim by a word-association test.

If the given words are *computer, copier, chocolate bar,* and *cola,* the four most associated words are *IBM, Xerox, Hershey's,* and *Coke.*

An astute leader will go one step further to solidify its position. Heinz owns the word *ketchup*. But Heinz went on to isolate the most important ketchup attribute. "Slowest ketchup in the West" is how the company preempted the thickness attribute. Owning the word *slow* helps Heinz maintain a 50 percent market share.

DON'T BE AFRAID TO BRAG

Despite all of the foregoing points about the power of being the perceived leader, we continue to come across leaders who don't want to talk about their leadership. Their response about avoiding this claim to what is rightfully theirs is often the same: "We don't want to brag."

Well, being a leader who doesn't brag is the best thing that can happen to your competition. When you've clawed your way to the top of the mountain, you had better plant your flag and take some pictures.

And besides, you can often find a nice way to express your leadership. One of our favorite leadership slogans does just that: "Fidelity Investments. Where 12 million investors put their trust."

If you don't take credit for your achievements, the one right behind you will find a way to claim what is rightfully yours.

What companies fail to appreciate is that leadership is a wonderful platform from which to tell the story of how you got to be number one. As we said earlier, people will believe whatever you say if they perceive you as a leader.

DIFFERENT FORMS OF LEADERSHIP

Leadership comes in many flavors, any of which can provide an effective way to differentiate yourself. Here's a quick sampling of different ways to claim leadership:

- *Sales leadership*. The strategy most often used by leaders is to proclaim how well their products sell. The Toyota Camry is the bestselling car in America. But others can claim their own sales leadership by carefully counting sales in different ways. Chrysler's Dodge Caravan is the top-selling minivan. The Ford Explorer is the top sport utility vehicle. This approach works because people tend to buy what others buy.

43

- *Technology leadership.*   Some companies with long histories of technological breakthroughs can use this form of leadership as a differentiator. In Austria, the rayon fiber manufacturer Lenzing isn't the sales leader, but it is the "world's leader in viscose fiber technology." The company pioneered many of the industry's breakthroughs in new and improved forms of rayon.

- *Performance leadership.*   Companies have products that aren't big sellers but are big performers. This can also be used as a way to separate yourself from competitors that can't perform at your level. Silicon Graphics is such a company. The company features visual workstations that make those Hollywood special effects possible, and high-powered wideband servers that handle graphics and data better than most. As a result, it's the "world's leader in high-performance computing." This approach works because companies with money often want the best, even if they don't need it.

HERITAGE IS A DIFFERENTIATING IDEA

In Chapter 2, we discussed the fact that minds are insecure. And any strategy that helps people overcome their insecurities is a good one.

Heritage has the power to make your product stand out. It can be a powerful differentiating idea, because there appears to be a natural psychological importance attached to having a long history, one that makes people feel secure in making a choice.

When we started to study why this is so, we assumed that having been around a long time suggested that a company knew what it was doing. People figured that it must have been doing something right.

But unlike countries such as China and Japan, where elders are given the utmost respect, our culture tends to have an abhorrence of old age. Everybody wants to be young. Old and wise means out of it and passé.

THE PSYCHOLOGY OF HERITAGE
When we asked Dr. Carol Moog why heritage is meaningful, the consumer psychologist made the following observations:

> *The psychological importance of heritage may derive from the power of being a participant in a continuous line that connects and bonds one to the right to be alive, to a history that one carries forward from the living past, through death and on into the next generation. The link is a link to immortality. Without a sense of heritage, of known ancestors, people are vulnerable*

> *to feeling isolated, abandoned, emotionally cut off, and ungrounded. Without a line from the past, it is difficult to believe in a line to the future.*

While that's all very heavy, another way to look at this approach is to recognize that dealing with a company that's been around a long time also gives prospects the feeling that they are dealing with an industry leader. If not the biggest in the industry, it certainly is a leader in longevity.

It's no wonder that marketers display their tradition and culture as a way of telling you why they are different.

BRING HERITAGE FORWARD

But tradition isn't always enough, says an Associated Press business writer. "Companies of all stripes have spent recent years devising new marketing tactics that blend consumer-comforting tradition with the progressiveness that's crucial to continued success."

Wells Fargo Bank, of Pony Express and stagecoach beginnings, takes its original idea and makes it relevant by simply stating, "Fast then. Fast now." The difference is that today's stagecoaches travel at the speed of light via advanced computer networks.

L.L. Bean jazzes up its catalog, goes online, and introduces women's clothing—while carefully maintaining its New England image. Says a company spokesperson, "You take the classic appeal and you take it to another generation."

The continued success of Tabasco in the pepper sauce business is an example of the balance between honoring your heritage and looking forward.

Its advertising strikes traditional themes such as down-home Louisiana bayous and pepper mash aged in oak barrels. But the company also presents itself as with-it and trendy, with Tabasco neckties, Cajun cooking festivals, and new Tabasco-laced drinks that originated in rural Louisiana oyster bars.

One popular drink is the prairie fire, which combines a shot of tequila with a splash of Tabasco.

"There are all sorts of balancing acts needed in marketing," says company president Paul C. P. McIlhenny.

Well said. He's balancing the old with the new.

FAMILY HERITAGE

In a world that's seeing the big get bigger, an effective way to separate yourself from the striving herd is to keep your business a family business. While taxes and ensuing generations don't always make this easy, family heritage can be a powerful concept if the family can be held together.

People seem to feel more kindly toward a family-run business as opposed to a cold, impersonal public corporation that's beholden to a bunch of greedy stockholders. Family members can be just as greedy. But, because what goes on is never reported, all that greed is kept behind closed doors.

Family businesses are also believed to be more involved with their product than with their stock price. They also are given higher marks for community involvement, because the family members tend to be natives of the town where the company was founded. We've also discovered that family businesses tend to treat their employees more like family. There's a feeling of having grown up together.

HOW A PRODUCT IS MADE CAN BE A DIFFERENTIATING IDEA

Companies tend to work very hard in developing new products. Hordes of engineers, designers, and manufacturing people spend endless hours producing and testing what they feel is a unique product that does its job better than anything in the market.

But all that work is often taken for granted by the marketing folks, who get swept away in their own activities, such as advertising, packaging, and promotion.

We're great believers in digging into a product to find out exactly how it works. More times than not we find a powerful differentiation idea that has been ignored.

THE MAGIC INGREDIENT

Many products contain a piece of technology or a design that makes them function. Often, this technology is patented. Yet marketing people tend to dismiss these elements as too complex or too confusing to explain to customers. They would rather conduct research and focus on the benefits or the lifestyle experience of the product. Their favorite speech goes like this: "People don't care how it's made. They only care about what it does for them."

The problem with this point of view is that in many categories, a number of products do the same thing for people. All toothpastes prevent cavities. All new cars drive very nicely. All detergents clean clothes. It's how they are made that often makes them different.

This is why we like to focus on the product and locate that unique piece of technology. Then, if possible, we give that design element a name, and if we can package it as a magic ingredient, all the better.

When Procter & Gamble introduced Crest toothpaste with fluoride for cavity prevention, the ad campaign made sure everyone knew it contained "fluoristan." Did anyone understand what that was? Nope. Did it matter? Nope. It just sounded impressive.

When Sony began its dominance in television, it made a fuss about the "Trinitron" picture tube. Did anyone understand what it was? Nope. Did it matter? Nope. It just sounded impressive.

General Motors has probably spent over $100 million promoting the Northstar system used in Cadillacs. Does anyone understand how this engine works? Nope. Does it matter? Nope. It just sounds impressive.

Magic ingredients don't have to be explained, because they are magic.

MAKING IT THE RIGHT WAY

Often, there is a wrong way and a right way to make a product. The wrong (or less desirable) way is often introduced as a money-saving process. Consultants like to call this "improving manufacturing practices" (translation: cutting costs). The right way absorbs the higher costs so as to produce a better product.

There are times, if an industry is going the wrong way, when you can be different by going the right way. Such was the case for Stanislaus Food Products. The company has become the leading manufacturer of tomato sauce for a large number of America's Italian restaurants. And it has accomplished this while charging higher prices. The winning strategy was not to follow the industry into concentrated tomato sauce (which is cheaper to make and to ship).

Dino Cortopassi, the owner of the company, felt that the fresh-packed method, in which the sauce was never put through the concentration process, was a better way to make this product. It costs more, but the sauce tastes better.

That's his difference. And much to his competitors' dismay, most of the real Italian restaurants in America agree with him.

MAKING IT THE OLD-FASHIONED WAY

A similar story comes from Aron Streit Inc., the last independent matzo company. (For those who aren't sure, *matzo* is the authentic, unleavened, unsalted, and un–everything else bread that kept the Israelites alive on their flight from Egypt.)

Even though the company has only a small share of a market dominated by B. Manischewitz, the Streit's Matzo folks realize that *tradition* is about all that distinguishes one matzo from another. Despite all the trendy outsourcing for many of its other products, Streit's still makes its matzos on Rivington Street in lower Manhattan—the same place where the company has made them since 1914.

If you go to Streit's Web site, Streitsmatzos.com, you'll discover that the company knows what the difference is all about. Here's how Streit's puts it: "Why is Streit's Matzo different from other domestic matzo brands? Because Streit's bakes only Streit's Matzo in our own ovens."

They still make their matzo the old-fashioned way.

HOTNESS IS A WAY TO DIFFERENTIATE

When you're hot, the world should know you're hot. As you saw in Chapter 2, people are like sheep. That's why they love to know what's hot and what's not. It's also why word of mouth is such a powerful force in marketing. That word of mouth usually consists of one person telling another person what's hot. This is important, for while America loves underdogs, people bet on the winners.

FEAR OF BOASTING

Unfortunately, many companies are shy in telling the world about their success. First they say that boasting isn't nice. It's pushy. It's bad manners. But what's really behind this reluctance is a fear that they won't stay hot forever. And then what? Won't they be embarrassed?

What I'm trying to explain is that getting a company or product off the ground is like launching a satellite. What you often need is some early thrust to get you into orbit. After that, it's a different game.

Being hot or experiencing sales growth beyond that of your competitors can give you the thrust you need to get your brand up to altitude. Once there, you can figure out something else to keep you there.

MANY WAYS TO BE HOT

When you're using a "hotness" strategy, you have the opportunity to define why you're hot. What many don't realize is that there are many ways to structure that definition. Here's a roundup of the most popular ways:

- *Sales.* The most often used approach is to compare your sales to your competitors' sales. But don't think you have to compare *annual* sales. You can use any time period you choose: 6 months, 2 years, 5 years. The time you choose to measure is the one that makes you look best. Remember that you are free to pick the parameters. Also, you don't have to compare yourself to your competitors. You can compare yourself to yourself.

- *Industry ratings.* Most industries have annual ratings for performance. They could be administered by industry magazines such as *Restaurant News* or consumer magazines such as *U.S. News & World Report* or organizations such as J.D. Powers. If you win a rating from one of these, use it as aggressively as possible.

• *Industry experts.* Some industries have experts or
  critics who are often quoted or who write widely
  read columns. This is especially true in the high-
  tech world, where you have Esther Tyson and the
  Gartner Group, for example. Sometimes you can
  use their quotes or reports as a way to define your
  success. Hollywood uses this device to establish
  a hot movie, as does the publishing world for a
  hot book.

THE PRESS CAN MAKE YOU HOT

While it's helpful to blow your own horn, it's even better if
you can get someone else to do it. This is where an aggressive public relations program can pay big dividends.

What's afoot here is the fact that "third-party" credentials are very powerful. Whether the third party is
your neighbor or your local newspaper, people feel that
these sources are unbiased. So when they say you're hot,
you must indeed be hot.

Creating a success in public relations is like throwing
a rock into a pond. The circles start small but spread
throughout the pond. You start with the experts, spread
to the trade papers, and expand out to the business and
consumer press.

But before you talk to the press, you've got to work
out your program. Here are all the steps.

Step 1: Make sense in the context.   Arguments are never made in a vacuum. There are always surrounding competitors trying to make arguments of their own. Your message has to make sense in the context of the category. It has to start with what the marketplace has heard and registered from your competition.

Step 2: Find the differentiating idea.   To be different is to be not the same. To be unique is to be one of a kind. So you're looking for something that separates you from your competitors. The secret to this is understanding that your differentness does not have to be product related. But it should set up a benefit for your customer.

Step 3: Have the credentials.   To build a logical argument for your difference, you must have the credentials to support your differentiating idea, to make it real and believable.

If you have a product difference, then you should be able to demonstrate that difference. The demonstration, in turn, supplies your credentials. If you have a leak-proof valve, then you should be able to have a direct comparison with valves that can leak.

Claims of difference without proof are really just claims.

Step 4: Communicate your difference. Just as you can't keep your light under a basket, you can't keep your difference under wraps.

If you build a differentiated product, the world will not automatically beat a path to your door. Better products don't win. Better perceptions tend to be the winners. Truth will not out unless it has some help along the way.

Every aspect of your communications should reflect your difference:

- Your advertising
- Your brochures
- Your Web site
- Your sales presentations

SUMMATION
....

**If you don't have
a point of difference,
you'd better have a low price.**

Strategy Is
All about Competition

As you just read in Chapter 3, you start your strategic planning with your competition in mind. Where are they strong? Where are they weak? The reason you start this way is because business today is not about reengineering or continuous improvement. Business is about *war*. It's not about better people and better products.

THE "BETTER PEOPLE" FALLACY

It's easy enough to convince your own staff that better people will prevail, even against the odds. It's what they want to hear. And surely, in a marketing war, quality is a factor as well as quantity.

It is, but superiority of force is such an overwhelming advantage that it overcomes most quality differences.

We have no doubt that the poorest team in the National Football League could consistently beat the best team in the NFL if it could field 12 men against the opposition's 11.

In business, where the teams are much larger, the ability to amass a quality difference is much more difficult to achieve.

The clear-thinking manager won't confuse the pep talk at a sales rally with the reality of the marketing arena. A good general never makes military strategy based on having better personnel. Nor should a business general.

Tell your people how terrific they are, but don't plan on winning the battle with superior personnel.

Count on winning the battle with a superior strategy.

Yet many companies cling deeply to the better people strategy. They're convinced they can recruit and hire substantially better people than the competition can, and that their better training programs can help them keep their "people" edge.

Any student of statistics would laugh at this belief. Sure, it's possible to put together a small cadre of superior people. But the larger the company, the more likely the average employee will be average.

And when it comes to the megacompanies, the possibility of assembling an intellectually superior team becomes statistically almost zero.

THE "BETTER PRODUCT" FALLACY

Another fallacy ingrained in the minds of most managers is the belief that the better product will win the marketing battle.

Behind the thinking of many marketing managers is the idea that "truth will out."

In other words, if you have the "facts" on your side, it's only necessary to find a good advertising agency that can communicate those facts to the prospect and a good sales force that can close the sale.

We call this approach *inside-out thinking*—the idea that somehow the advertising agency or the sales force can take the truth, as the company knows it, and use this truth to clear up the misconceptions that reside inside the mind of the prospect.

Don't be fooled. Misconceptions cannot easily be changed by an advertising or sales effort.

What is truth? Inside every human being is a little black box. When a human being is exposed to your advertising or sales claim, that person looks inside the box and says "That's right" or "That's wrong."

The single most wasteful thing you can do in marketing today is to try to change a human mind. Once a mind is made up, it's almost impossible to change.

What is truth? Truth is the perception that's inside the mind of the prospect. It may not be your truth, but it's the only truth you can work with. You have to accept that truth and then deal with it.

IF YOU'RE SO SMART, HOW COME YOU'RE NOT RICH?

Even if you succeed in convincing the prospect that you have a better product, the prospect soon has a second thought: "Hey, if your computer is better than IBM's, how come you're not the leader, like IBM is?"

Even if you get a few black boxes to go along with you, the owners of those black boxes soon let the unsold majority sway their judgment.

If you're so smart, how come you're not rich? That's a tough question to answer. In a marketing war, you can't win just by being right.

There's the illusion, of course, that over the long run, the better product will win. But history, military and marketing, is written by the winners, not the losers.

Might is right. Winners always have the better product, and they're always available to say so.

MARKETING AS WAR

Al Ries and I first presented this observation more than 25 years ago in a book titled *Marketing Warfare*. In hindsight, this book was published in the dark ages of competition. A decade ago, the term *global economy* wasn't talked about very much. The vast array of technology that we take for granted was still a glimmer in the eyes of some Silicon Valley engineers. Global commerce was pretty much limited to a handful of multinational companies.

As we entered the new millennium, of the world's 100 largest economies, 51 were not countries but corporations. The 500 largest accounted for a stunning 70 percent of world trade.

Today's marketplace makes the one we first wrote about look like a tea party. The wars are escalating and breaking out in every part of the globe. Everyone is after everyone's business everywhere.

All this means that the principles of *Marketing Warfare* are more important than ever. Companies must learn how to deal with their competitors—how to avoid their strengths and how to exploit their weaknesses.

Organizations must learn that it's not about do or die for your company. It's about making the other guy die for his company.

A CHANGE OF PHILOSOPHY

The classic definition of *marketing* leads one to believe that marketing has to do with satisfying consumer needs and wants.

Marketing is "human activity directed at satisfying needs and wants through exchange processes," says Philip Kotler of Northwestern University.

Marketing is "the performance of those activities which seek to accomplish an organization's objectives by anticipating customer or client needs and directing a flow or need-satisfying goods and services from producer to customer or client," says E. Jerome McCarthy of Michigan State University.

Marketing people traditionally have been customer-oriented. Over and over again they have warned management to be customer- rather than production-oriented.

Ever since World War II, King Customer has reigned supreme in the world of marketing.

But it's beginning to look like King Customer is dead. And marketing people have been selling a corpse to top management.

That's because today, every company is customer-oriented. Knowing what the customer wants isn't too helpful if a dozen other companies are already serving the same customer. General Motor's problem is not the customer. General Motor's problem is Ford, Chrysler, and the imports.

BECOMING COMPETITOR-ORIENTED

To be successful, a company must become competitor-oriented. It must look for weak points in the positions of its competitors and then launch marketing attacks against those weak points.

There are those who would say that a well-thought-out marketing plan always includes a section on the competition. Indeed it does. Usually toward the back of the plan in a section titled "Competitive Evaluation." The major part of the plan usually spells out the details of the marketplace, its various segments, and a myriad of customer research statistics carefully gleaned from endless focus groups, test panels, and concept and marketing tests.

In the marketing plan of the future, many more pages will be dedicated to the competition. This plan will carefully dissect each participant in the marketplace. It will develop a list of competitive weaknesses and strengths as well as a plan of action to either exploit or defend against them.

There might even come a day when this plan will contain a dossier on each of the competitors' key marketing people, which will include their favorite tactics and style of operation (not unlike the documents the Germans kept on Allied commanders in World War II).

What does all this portend for marketing people of the future?

It means they'll have to be prepared to wage marketing warfare. More and more, successful marketing campaigns will have to be planned like military campaigns.

Strategic planning will become more and more important. Companies will have to learn how to *attack* and to *flank* their competition, how to *defend* their positions, and how and when to wage *guerrilla* warfare. They will need better intelligence on how to anticipate competitive moves.

It's all about pursuing the right competitive strategy. It's all about understanding the four types of marketing warfare shown in the accompanying diagram "the strategic square" and figuring out which applies to your situation.

These principles constitute a very simple strategic model for company survival in the twenty-first century. Let's review and update them.

1. *Defensive warfare is what market leaders wage.*
   Leadership is reserved for those companies whose

The Strategic Square

Defensive Warfare	Offensive Warfare
Flanking Warfare	Guerrilla Warfare

customers perceive them as the leader. (Not as pretenders to being leaders.)

Your most aggressive leaders are willing to attack themselves with new ideas. We have long used Gillette as a classic defender. Every 2 or 3 years it replaces its existing blade with a new idea. We've had two-bladed razors (Atra). We've had shock-absorbent razors (Sensor). And now we have three-bladed razors (Mach 3). A rolling company gathers few competitors.

An aggressive leader always blocks competitive moves. When Bic introduced the disposable razor, Gillette quickly countered with the twin-bladed disposable (Good News). It now dominates this category.

All this adds up to over 60 percent of the blade market. That's a leader.

2. *Offensive warfare is the strategy for the number-two or -three business in a category.* The first principle is to avoid the strength of the leader's position. What you want to do is find a weakness and attack at that point. Then you focus all your efforts at that point.

In recent years, the fastest-growing pizza chain in America has been Papa John's Pizza. Papa John's attacked Pizza Hut at its weak point, ingredients. John Schnatter, the founder, got his hands on the best tomato sauce in the country. It was a sauce that the other chains couldn't buy. This became the cornerstone of his concept: "Better Ingredients. Better Pizza."

Schnatter has stayed narrowly focused on the better-ingredients concept in everything he uses, such as cheese and toppings. He even filters the water for better dough.

As the *Wall Street Journal* reported, "Papa John's is on a tear." This is not the kind of news that Pizza Hut is very happy about.

One of the best ways of attacking a leader is with a new-generation technology.

In the land of paper making, quality control systems have become a two-horse race between Measurex, the current leader, and AccuRay (a part of Asea Brown Boveri), the former leader in systems that measure the uniformity of paper as it is produced.

AccuRay attacked Measurex with a new generation of electronic scanning technology that measures the entire sheet instead of just parts of the sheet. This new weapon is called Hyper Scan Full Sheet Imaging, and it promises a quality control measurement that Measurex can't measure up to. This idea will work because AccuRay just made its competitor obsolete.

3. *New or smaller players that are trying to get a foothold in a category by avoiding the main battle pursue flanking warfare.* This strategy usually involves a move into an uncontested area and includes the element of surprise. Often it's a new idea, such as gourmet popping corn (Orville Redenbacher) or Dijon mustard (Grey Poupon).

A brilliant flanking move has been under way in the golf world. While others have focused on drivers, irons, and putters, Adams Golf has gone into an area that has never been heavily contested. (It lies in the fairway about 200 yards from the green.)

Adams's flanking move was to introduce a patented flat design of fairway woods that were perfect for those tight lies. The simple but brilliant product name says it all: Tight Lies Fairway Woods.

67

Very quickly, they became the fastest-growing fairway woods in the country.

When a 19-year-old named Michael Dell started his own little computer company, he knew he couldn't compete with established companies for floor space in stores. However, the rules of the industry, at that time, dictated that computers had to be sold in stores. Every company in the industry believed that customers wouldn't trust a mail-order company to provide such a high-end item.

Dell broke the rule. He flanked the industry with direct marketing. And he built an $800 million company in 5 years.

4. *Guerrilla warfare is often the land of the smaller companies.*   The first principle is to find a market small enough to defend. It's the big fish in the small pond strategy.

No matter how successful you become, never act like a leader. Going big-time is what does in successful guerrilla companies. (Anyone remember People's Express Airlines?)

Finally, you have to be prepared to bug out at a moment's notice. Small companies can't afford to take those losses. Melt into the jungle so you can live to fight another day.

One of the most interesting guerrilla case studies is under way down in the Caribbean. This is where the tourism wars are being waged by all the islands, big and small.

Grenada is one of the southernmost islands in the Caribbean. Famous for President Reagan's invasion to expel a few Cubans, Grenada is now trying to get a share of the tourist business.

Because it's late in the game, the island is unspoiled. There is little concrete, and there are no overdeveloped beaches. In fact, there are no buildings higher than a palm tree. That has enabled Grenada to develop a strategy of being the unspoiled island, or "the Caribbean the way it used to be."

This is a defensible idea, because all the other islands are developed. There's no way they can suddenly become unspoiled.

But smaller jungle fighters must be aware of the fact that the jungle can become an overpopulated place. Such was the case for microbrewers, the successful guerrillas in the beer wars.

Tantalized by consumer fancy for every imaginable new concoction, and with easy access to capital, micros churned out as many as 4000 different brands. With that many guerrillas in a small market, you end up just killing off each other, which is exactly what happened.

After meteoric growth, the microbrew industry has gone about as flat as day-old beer. Now, a full-fledged shakeout is on tap among brewers and brewpubs.

Who will survive the pub brawl? Many industry executives speculate that among the survivors will be Sam Adams, the only micro with a truly national franchise, and long-time California micros Sierra Nevada and Anchor Steam.

TACTICS AND STRATEGY

After years of strategic work for some of America's largest companies, I have come to a revolutionary conclusion: Strategy should be developed from the bottom up, not from the top down. In other words, strategy should be developed from a deep knowledge of and involvement in the actual tactics of the business itself.

Tactics should dictate strategies. That is, the communications tactic should dictate the marketing strategy.

Most marketing people believe the reverse. The accepted wisdom is that the grand strategy of the organization should be set first; then the tactics can follow.

That's because most managers are obsessed with what they want to do. What are long-term plans except a meticulous outline of where managers want their company to be in 5 or 10 years?

When you put the emphasis on strategy, or where you want to be in the years ahead, you commit one of the two cardinal sins of business: (1) the refusal to accept failure and (2) the reluctance to exploit success. It's what can be called *top-down thinking*.

To better understand this requires some new definitions that Al Ries and I laid out in our book *Bottom-Up Marketing*.

WHAT'S A TACTIC?

A tactic is an idea. When you look for a tactic, you are looking for an idea.

But the notion of an idea is a nebulous one. What kind of idea? *Where* do you find one? These are the initial questions that must be answered.

In order to help you answer these questions, we propose using the following specific definition: *A tactic is a competitive mental angle*.

A tactic must have a *competitive angle* in order to have a chance of success. This does not necessarily mean a better product or service, but rather there must be an element of differentness. It could be smaller, bigger, lighter, heavier, cheaper, or more expensive. It could be a different distribution system.

71

Furthermore, the tactic must be competitive in the total marketing arena, not just competitive in relation to one or two other products or services.

A competitive mental *angle* is the point in the mind that allows your marketing program to work effectively. That's the point you must leverage to achieve results.

But a tactic is not enough. To complete the process, you need to turn the tactic into a strategy. (If the tactic is a nail, the strategy is a hammer.) You need both to establish a position in the mind.

WHAT'S A STRATEGY?

A strategy is not a goal. Like life itself, a strategy ought to be focused on the journey, not the goal. Top-down thinkers are goal-oriented. They first determine what it is they want to achieve, and then they try to devise ways and means to achieve their goals.

But most goals are simply not achievable. Goal-setting tends to be an exercise in frustration. Marketing, like politics, is the art of the possible.

In our definition, a strategy is not a goal. It's a *coherent marketing direction.*

A strategy is *coherent* in the sense that it is focused on the tactic that has been selected.

A strategy encompasses coherent *marketing* activities. Product, pricing, distribution, advertising—all the

72

activities that make up the marketing mix must be coherently focused on the tactic.

(Think of the tactic as a particular wavelength of light and the strategy as a laser tuned to that wavelength. You need both to penetrate the mind of the prospect.)

Finally, a strategy is a coherent marketing *direction*. Once the strategy is established, the direction shouldn't be changed.

The purpose of the strategy is to mobilize your resources to preempt the tactic. By committing all your resources to one strategic direction, you maximize the exploitation of the tactic without the limitation that the existence of a goal implies.

In marketing, as in warfare, the safest strategy is rapid exploitation of the tactic. Rest is for losers. Winners keep the pressure on.

TACTICS VERSUS STRATEGY

A tactic is a singular idea or angle. A strategy has many elements, all of which are focused on the tactic.

A tactic is an angle that is unique or different. A strategy may well be mundane.

A tactic is independent of time and relatively constant. A strategy unfolds over a period of time. A sale is a tactic used at one time or another by most of the retailers in America. A store that has a sale every day is a discount store, which is a strategy.

A tactic is a competitive advantage. A strategy is designed to maintain that competitive advantage.

A tactic is external to the product, service, or company. It may not even be a product the company makes. A strategy is internal. (Strategies often require a great deal of internal reorganization.)

A tactic is communications-oriented. A strategy is product-, service-, or company-oriented.

The principle of bottom-up marketing is simple: You work from the specific to the general, from the short term to the long term.

Note, too, the singular implication of bottom-up marketing. Find a tactic that will work, and then build it into a strategy. Find one tactic, not two or three or four.

Generally speaking, that tactic is one thing in which you are very skilled as compared to your competitors. In World War II, General George S. Patton was very skilled in tank warfare. That was his tactic. Herb Kelleher, of Southwest Airlines, was very skilled in short-haul air travel, which all leads to specialization.

SUMMATION

**Know your competition.
Avoid their strength.
Exploit their weakness.**

Strategy Is
All about Specialization

If business is war, the way to survive and prosper is to be better than your competitors at one thing. Whether you're big or whether you're small, your chosen strategy should revolve around what is often called your *core competency*. Why is that so important?

It's because people are impressed with those who concentrate on a specific activity or product. They perceive them as experts. And as experts, people tend to give them credit for more knowledge and experience than they sometimes deserve. This isn't surprising when you consider the definition of *expert:* "one having much training and knowledge in some special field."

Conversely, the generalist is rarely given credit for expertise in many fields of endeavor no matter how good he or she may be. Common sense tells the prospect that a single person or company cannot be expert in everything.

A LESSON LEARNED

Many years ago at General Electric, I learned the power of the specialist over the generalist.

At the time, GE was launching a concept called the *turnkey power plant*. The concept was simple. The GE folks would go to an electric utility with their ability to put all the pieces together. At the end of the process, they would give the utility the keys to the complete plant. (A one-stop shopping concept.)

Nice idea, right? Wrong.

The utility said, "Thank you very much. We'll give you the contract for the turbine generators; other specialists will get the contracts for the controls, switch gear, et cetera."

Even though it was General Electric, the inventor of electricity, the utilities wanted the best of the breed: the specialists.

ANOTHER LESSON LEARNED

Well, GE figured, those utility guys think they know everything. Let's go to the lady of the house and offer her a "GE kitchen."

It was no different. The lady of the house said, "Thank you very much. We'll take your refrigerator; but we'll get the KitchenAid dishwasher, the Maytag washing machine, et cetera."

Even though it was General Electric, the big kahuna in appliances, the lady of the house wanted to pick what she thought was the best.

Generalists like General Electric, though their names are big, are weak in the market.

Consider a big food name like Kraft. When that name is taken out against specialist brand names, nothing good happens. In mayonnaise, Hellmann's trounces it. In jellies, Smucker's kills it. In mustard, French's annihilates it. In yogurt, Dannon destroys it.

Luckily for Kraft, it has some specialist brands of its own. In fact, Kraft's biggest brand is one that few people recognize as a Kraft product. It's Philadelphia brand cream cheese. Even though "Kraft" is on the package, people don't even see it. To most, it's all about those little cheesemakers in Philadelphia.

THE SAME GOES FOR RETAIL

Take the retail industry. Which retailers are in trouble today? The department stores. And what's a department store? A place that sells everything. That's a recipe for disaster, because it's very hard to differentiate an "everything" place.

Campeau, L.J. Hooker, and Gimbel's all wound up in bankruptcy court. Hills department stores also went bankrupt. Macy's, the world's largest store, filed for bankruptcy. While some department stores have emerged intact, this indicates how tough the world is becoming for this kind of store.

Interstate Department Stores also went bankrupt. So the company looked at the books and decided to focus on the only product it made money on: toys. As long as Interstate was going to focus on toys, it decided to change its name to Toys "R" Us. Today Toys "R" Us does 17 percent of the retail toy business in the country.

Many retail chains are successfully patterning themselves on the Toys "R" Us formula: a narrow focus with in-depth stock. Staples and Blockbuster Video are examples.

In the retail field generally, the big successes are the specialists:

- *The Limited.* Upscale clothing for working women.
- *The Gap.* Casual clothing for the young at heart.
- *Benetton.* Wool and cotton clothing for young swingers.
- *Victoria's Secret.* Sexy undergarments.
- *Foot Locker.* Athletic shoes.
- *Banana Republic.* Upmarket casual wear.

When a clothing chain with a name like Banana Republic can be successful, you know we live in the age of the specialist.

THE COUNTERPOINT TO GROWTH

Economist Milton Friedman said it perfectly: "We don't have a desperate need to grow. We have a desperate desire to grow." We all have watched that in action as company after company decided that bigger was better. Now we are clearly seeing that bigness has a lot of problems. It's harder to manage. There is no focus, and it all becomes a numbers game. Most bad marketing is driven by that desire, which is in turn driven by Wall Street, which is in turn driven by greed. (More in Chapter 8.)

The counter to all this is *specialization*. It is a very effective way to compete with larger, unfocused, we-do-everything competitors. The reason: As mentioned earlier, customers don't think a company can be good at everything. And, very often, they want to buy the best of the breed. Consider the current plight of the airline industry. Only one company is making money. It's Southwest Airlines, the specialist in short-haul, point-to-point air travel. No hubs, no food, no reserved seats, and only one kind of airplane.

Specialization lines up with where the world is going. There will be big global brands that will be successful, and there will be highly specialized brands doing very well in their part of the jungle. The companies in trouble will be those in the mushy middle. They won't be big enough to compete globally. Nor will they be flexible enough to compete with the smaller specialists.

BECOMING THE EXPERT

The specialist has a chance to nail down a field of expertise as a differentiator.

In the business of environmental consulting, there are a lot of players, big and small, all of whom are doing pretty much the same thing. A company in Boston called ENSR has come up with a unique field of expertise: environmental due diligence. In other words, when an international real estate or business transaction takes place, this company offers to use its global resources to evaluate the environmental aspects of the deal. That specialty not only differentiates it from its competitors, but sets the company up to come back and solve the problems its work has uncovered.

A PUBLISHER'S DREAM

Unless you're an automobile buff, you've probably never heard of a monthly magazine called *Hemmings Motor News*. But this may be the ultimate specialist success in publishing, where expertise in a given field is the holy grail.

Hemmings sells 265,000 copies a month. It grosses $20 million a year. A typical issue runs 800 pages and is crammed with 20,000 advertisements, offering everything from a wheel bearing set for a Model T Ford (yours for $55) to a 1932 Rolls-Royce Henley roadster (a steal at $650,000).

The bulk of the magazine consists of small black-and-white classified ads, prepaid by check or credit card. The editorial content is miniscule. The sales department is miniscule.

Terry Ehrich, the owner of one of publishing's great cash cows, says the magazine has ridden the popularity of car collecting and car restoring.

"I'm just a mediocre jockey on a helluva horse," he says. A horse that happens to be a helluva specialist idea.

BECOMING GENERIC

The ultimate weapon for a specialist is to become generic. This is where your brand name represents the product as well as the category.

Gatorade is a very powerful specialist that has reached that level in sports drinks.

While it's not easy to become a Xerox in copiers or a Scotch in tapes, the specialist has a chance to hit what is the highest level in brand success.

One of my favorite generic specialists is Martin-Baker Aircraft Company in Highes Denham, England. With only 1000 employees, it is a family-owned company that pioneered the ejection seat for military jet aircraft.

Almost every such aircraft has one of these high-technology seats to catapult its occupant clear in an emergency. These seats cost up to $150,000 apiece, and Martin-Baker has produced over 70,000 of them. That's more than three times the production of its nearest rival.

I happened to spend some years in naval aviation, and that seat is always referred to as a *Martin-Baker seat*.

OTHER SMALL SPECIALISTS

While many folks read about icons in trouble and the difficulties of the global economy in maintaining market share, there are some companies that you never read about that are doing very well, thank you.

Landauer is a company that makes radiation badges for X-ray workers. It does $58 million in sales and has a net income of 28 percent of revenue. That's a 50 percent market share. Its specialization strategy: Stay in a small market that doesn't fit well with bigger companies.

Zebra Technologies makes thermal printers used in barcode labeling. It does $475 million in sales, nets $71 million, and has a 35 percent market share. Its specialization strategy: Develop a unique distribution network into hundreds of industrial niches that is not easily identified by competitors.

Aftermarket Technology remanufactures transmissions. It does $415 million in sales and has a 72 percent market share of dealer-installed, remanufactured transmissions for cars made by the Big Three automakers. Its specialization strategy: maintaining its expertise.

There are many small but very happy guerrillas in the jungle out there.

BIG SPECIALISTS

Specialists are often big companies in disguise. People don't realize that they are specialists. Here are three such companies.

3M Company is a $16 billion company that likes to talk about its thousands of innovative products. But in my view, what drives this company is its basic expertise in sticking things together with adhesives and fasteners. No one does it better. Products such as overhead projection systems, silicone breast implants, data storage, audio and videotape, copiers, and heart-surgery equipment were all losers and are gone. Its specialties, like Post-it Notes and Scotch tape, roll on.

Gillette is an $8 billion company that is the Godzilla of razor blades, with a worldwide share of more than 60 percent. That is its specialty. While it also owns Duracell batteries, Braun appliances, and Oral-B dental-care products, these are really only sideshows to its basic shaving business. Gillette has sold its hair-care business as well as stationary products and should probably exit anything that doesn't give you a close shave.

Otis is the world's number-one maker of elevators, with over 1 million in service around the world. It is also United Technologies' most successful division, which points to an interesting strategy. If you want to be very big, do what United Technologies has done. Own a number of specialist companies, such as an air-conditioning specialist (Carrier), a helicopter specialist (Sikorsky), a jet engine specialist (Pratt & Whitney), and a defense electronics specialist (Norden). United Technologies is a very big multi-specialty corporation that does very well around the world.

NOW THE BAD NEWS

A successful specialist has to stay specialized. You can't begin to chase other business, because you'll begin to erode your prospect's perceptions of your being a specialist.

Heart surgeons know this instinctively. They don't decide to go after knee replacements just because they've become a big business.

Most marketers don't like to be locked into one business or specialty. They want to be as many things as they can. What they don't realize is that as soon as they head out to be something else, they open the door for another company to become the specialist. Heinz was a specialist in pickles. Then it became a ketchup maker. Now it's just about out of a pickle business dominated by Vlasic and Mt. Olive.

In the U.S. market, Volkswagen was once the specialist in small cars. Then VW went big, fast, and recreational. Today the Japanese and Americans dominate this business.

Scott was America's number-one tissue brand, but then diversified into a raft of different paper products. Now Charmin is the leader in tissue.

BEWARE OF THE CEO'S HOBBY

Magna International is a specialist that is a major supplier of parts to the world's top automakers. It has clients the likes of Chrysler, Ford, Jeep, Dodge,

Chevrolet, Mercedes, and Cadillac. Its sales are around $6 billion per annum. It is at the forefront of the trend in the automotive industry that has suppliers delivering increasingly larger and more complex parts, such as entire seating systems.

But the company's chairman, Frank Stronach, is also an avid horse-racing fan who owns hundreds of horses. So it wasn't totally surprising that the company suddenly picked up some decidedly noncore assets, such as California's Santa Anita racetrack. (That's a horse of a different specialty.) Other tracks are under discussion.

Now he wants to move from auto parts to racetracks and sports-gambling operations. Well, it's also not surprising that a lot of shareholders aren't very happy.

My bet: nothing but trouble.

TELL IT LIKE IT IS

Don't make the assumption that everyone knows who the specialist is in a category. One of the things I advise is to position yourself as "the specialist in (whatever)."

People want to know this information because they want to know who the expert is in a business. And if that's all you do, make sure they know it's all you do.

Such was the case with Subaru, a Japanese car company that was having its problems. When George Muller became president in 1993, he asked, "What are we good at?" and "What's our persona?" The answer was all-wheel-drive technology.

Right then and there, he decided to focus on that specialty and, as he said, "We made a commitment to sell only all-wheel-drive to differentiate ourselves from Toyota and Honda."

And in its advertising, Subaru proudly announces that it doesn't make cars, it specializes in nothing but four-wheel-drive vehicles. It's a move that has turned around a me-too car company that was headed over a sales cliff. (Sales were down by 60 percent from their peak.) The company survived because it used a specialty to differentiate itself.

You'll notice that I haven't yet published a book on specialization. Well, hang on. Someday you'll probably see one titled *Specialize to Survive*. Until then, this chapter will have to suffice.

SUMMATION
••••••••••••••••••••••••

It's better to be exceptional at one thing than good at many things.

Strategy Is
All about Simplicity

Complex strategies such as complex battle plans are usually doomed to failure. There are too many things that can go wrong. The holy grail is simplicity. But here's the rub: most people admire complexity and don't trust something that's simple. It has no appeal to the imagination. It's a subject on which I spent a great deal of time when I cowrote *The Power of Simplicity*.

IN SEARCH OF THE OBVIOUS

The antidote for fear of simple ideas is common sense. Unfortunately, people often leave their common sense out in the parking lot when they come to work.

As Henry Mintzberg, professor of management at McGill University, said, "Management is a curious phenomenon. It is generously paid, enormously influential and significantly devoid of common sense."

Common sense is wisdom that is shared by all. It's something that registers as an obvious truth to a community.

Simple ideas tend to be obvious ideas because they have a ring of truth about them. But people distrust their instincts. They feel there must be a hidden, more complex answer. Wrong. What's obvious to you is obvious to many. That's why an obvious answer usually works so well in the marketplace.

If you look up the dictionary definition of *common sense*, you discover that it is native good judgment that is free from emotional bias or intellectual subtlety. It's also not dependent on special technical knowledge.

In other words, you are seeing things as they really are. You are following the dictates of cold logic, eliminating both sentiment and self-interest from your decision. Nothing could be simpler.

AN OBSERVATION FROM THE STREET

Consider this scenario. If you were to ask 10 people at random how well a Cadillac would sell if it looked like a

Chevrolet, just about all of them would say, "Not very well."

These people are using nothing but common sense in their judgment. They have no data or research to support their conclusion. They also have no technical knowledge or intellectual subtlety. To them, a Cadillac is a big expensive car, and a Chevrolet is a smaller inexpensive car. They are seeing things as they really are.

But at General Motors, rather than seeing the world as it is, those in charge would rather see it as they want it to be. Common sense is ignored—and so the Cimarron was born. Not surprisingly, it didn't sell very well. (And we're being kind.)

Was this a lesson learned? It doesn't appear so. GM came back with the Catera, another Cadillac that looked like a Chevrolet. Like its predecessor, it didn't sell very well because it made no sense. You know it and I know it. GM doesn't want to know it.

Leonardo da Vinci saw the human mind as a laboratory for gathering material from the eyes, ears, and other organs of perception—material that was then channeled through the organ of common sense. In other words, common sense is a sort of supersense that rides herd over our other senses. It's supersense that many in business refuse to trust.

Anyone who's hung around the marketing world for a while realizes that people are quite irrational at times. Right now, we're overrun by four-wheel-drive vehicles designed to travel off the road. Does anybody ever leave the road? Less than 10 percent. Do people need these vehicles? Not really. Why do they buy them? Because everyone else is buying them. How's that for "rational"?

Now some words about intellectual subtlety.

A company's strategy goes wrong when the company is conned by subtle research and arguments about where the world is headed. (Nobody really knows, but many make believe they know.) These views are carefully crafted and usually mixed in with some false assumptions disguised as facts.

RESEARCH CAN CONFUSE YOU

The question you're asking yourself is "Don't you believe in research?"

The answer is yes and no.

I believe in certain *kinds* of research. I also believe in not getting mesmerized by data, in not trusting your own instincts. To help with these likes and dislikes, let's return to the military analogy I employed in *Marketing Warfare.*

The parallels between war and marketing are numerous.

In business, the terrain is the marketplace. The enemy is the competition. The objective is the consumer's mind. The weapons are the media.

RESEARCH IS INTELLIGENCE

And the gathering of intelligence is known as *research*.

Good military brains are often suspicious of the intelligence reports they receive. (And rightly so.) So are many marketers.

The famous military historian Karl von Clausewitz put it this way: "A great part of the information obtained in war is contradictory, a still greater part is false, and by far the greatest part is of a doubtful character."

Can't live with it, can't live without it, you might say.

But whatever its intrinsic frustrations, intelligence gathering is continually broadening in scope. Companies such as GM, Kodak, and Motorola have established formal intelligence units to oversee their intelligence work. Other companies have made "business intelligence" and "competitor analysis" a key part of their strategic planning process.

America's 50 leading research organizations spend about $4 billion in search of answers. Thirty-eight percent comes from outside the United States.

These intelligence efforts are growing in direct proportion to competitive pressures.

A FUNDAMENTAL PARADOX

That's probably because of a fundamental paradox in human behavior. The more unpredictable the world becomes, the more we seek out and rely upon forecasts to determine what we should do. (The *California*

Management Review made this point in a landmark article titled "Management & Magic.")

Gone are the days when companies designed their strategies as if they had no competition. Gone are the strategic planners who crunched numbers, preached quantitative models, but ignored the guys who were pre- pared to eat their lunch. (When growth in many mar- kets stalled at the end of the 1990s while competition escalated, the grandiose strategies of the day suddenly weren't worth the paper they were printed on.)

So what's a marketer to do? How can you best use intelligence to make sound strategic decisions?

Here are some suggestions.

DON'T GET MESMERIZED
BY THE DATA

In our overconnected society, the problem is too much raw data, rather than not enough. In this kind of world, infor- mation isn't power. Simplicity is power. What you know is power only if you have the ability to separate the important from the billions of pieces of information swirling around you. Simplicity is the art of making the complex clear.

One of the pitfalls of the multi-billion-dollar market- ing research industry is that researchers don't get paid for simplicity. Instead, they seem to get paid by the pound.

The need is to filter out the overabundance of data and focus on the significant pieces. Usually, those represent less than 5 percent of your entire information inventory. A story may be in order.

The scene: The office of a brand manager at Procter & Gamble. My problem was what to do with one of their largest brands. I asked a simple question as to the availability of their research. Once again I was surprised by the answer: "Research? We've got a computer full of it. How do you want it? In fact, we've got so much of it that we don't know what to do with it."

A flood of data should never be allowed to wash away your common sense, and your own feeling for the market.

And remember that fads can masquerade as data. According to one market estimate in 1980, 5 percent of all U.S. households would be hooked into Videotext by 1985. But Videotext was the fad that never was. Knight-Ridder spent $60 million setting up a Videotext service that never made money and was ultimately abandoned. (Of course, the unforeseen winner was the Internet, which did indeed hook us all up to text.)

DON'T GET MESMERIZED BY FOCUS GROUPS

Focus groups are one of the most popular and misused research tools in the business. Allowing rooms full of total strangers with big mouths to influence your marketing strategy can be disastrous.

First of all, the process has been distorted. Have you ever wondered where the word *focus* came from? The concept was first used in the 1960s as a way to better focus the ensuing research on a subject. That's right, it was just the first step.

Yet today, many companies never get around to the quantitative research, based on a true sample of the target audience. They act on the opinions blurted out by those small groups of people.

Second, the process turns casual bystanders (or "bysitters") into marketing experts.

The average person doesn't think too deeply about anything much beyond money, sex, gossip, and body weight. The average person hasn't really *thought* about toothpaste for a total of 10 minutes in his or her lifetime, much less for the 2 hours of a toothpaste focus group. And yet, in a focus group, you're asking people to form opinions in a manner that goes way beyond that of their normal mental processing.

You're turning them into marketing managers for a day. They'll be only too happy to tell you how to run your business. The question is, should you *let* them?

FOCUS GROUPS ARE A POWDER KEG

They can blow up, and blow you off in the wrong direction.

Ask women about beauty products in a group setting, and typically they will deny any emotional involvement. Instead, they'll tell you what they think you want to hear. The same with men and automobiles.

Ask people to critique your strategies or your advertising, and they'll overstate their motivations and needs and understanding.

Focus groups are balky barometers of behavior. When a big packaged-goods company planned to introduce a squirtable soft-drink concentrate for kids, it held focus groups to watch the reaction. In the sessions, children squirted the product neatly into cups. But back home, few of the little rascals could resist the temptation to decorate the floors and walls with the colorful liquid. After a flood of complaints from parents, the product was withdrawn.

DON'T GET MESMERIZED BY TEST MARKETS

There's a Catch-22 factor at work in test markets. They are meant to forecast product performance, but results can be skewed by unforeseen events in the marketplace. Campbell Soup Company spent 18 months developing a blended fruit juice called Juiceworks. By the time it reached the market, three competing brands were already on store shelves. Campbell dropped the product.

When Crystal Pepsi (a clear cola) was test-marketed, it quickly moved to over a 4 share, and was just as quickly christened by the trade press as a success. Wrong. Several months later it plunged to a 1 share. What the marketing people forgot to factor in was the curiosity factor. People were curious about a clear cola, but then decided brown colas taste better. (No surprise.)

DON'T BELIEVE EVERYTHING THEY SAY

Researchers may promise to reveal attitudes, but attitudes aren't a reliable predictor of behavior. People often talk one way, but act another. Mark Twain said it brilliantly: "I think we never become really and genuinely our entire and honest selves until we are dead and then not until we've been dead years and years. People ought to start dead and then they would be honest so much earlier."

Many years ago, DuPont commissioned a study in which interviewers stopped 5000 women on their way into supermarkets and asked them what they expected to buy.

If you had gone to the bank on those findings alone, you would have been deeply in hock.

How come? Because the interviewers then checked the same women's purchases on their way out of the store. In terms of the product categories they had expected to purchase, only 3 out of 10 bought the specific brand they had said they would—7 out of 10 had bought other brands.

Another classic example is the research conducted before Xerox introduced the plain-paper copier. What came back was the conclusion that no one would pay 5 cents for a plain-paper copy when they could get a Thermofax copy for a cent and a half.

Xerox ignored the research, and the rest is history.

GET SOME SNAPSHOTS OF THE MIND

What you really want to get is a quick snapshot of the *perceptions* that exist in the mind. Not deep thoughts, not suggestions.

What you're after are the perceived strengths and weaknesses of you and your competitors, as they exist in the minds of the target group of consumers.

Our favorite mode of research is to line up the basic attributes that surround a category and then ask people to score them on a rating scale of 1 to 10. This is done on a competitor–competitor basis. The objective is to see who owns what idea or concept in a category.

Take toothpaste as an example. There are perhaps six attributes that surround this product: cavity prevention, taste, tooth whitening, breath protection, natural ingredients, and advanced technology. Crest built its brand on cavity protection, Aim on taste, UltraBrite on whitening, and Close-Up on breath protection. More recently, Tom's of Maine has preempted natural ingredients, and Mentadent has become a major player with its baking soda and peroxide technology.

Everyone owns an attribute.

The trick is to figure out in advance which attribute you would like to preempt in the mind. The research should serve as your road map into that mind, and around its perceptions of your competitors. (I discussed this earlier in Chapter 3.)

OWNING A WORD IN THE MIND

In *The 22 Immutable Laws of Marketing*, I wrote about the *law of focus*. A company can become incredibly successful if it can find a way to own a word in the mind of the prospect. Not a complicated word. Not an invented one. The simple words are best, words taken right out of the dictionary.

This is the law of focus. You burn your way into the mind by narrowing the focus to a single word or concept. It's the ultimate marketing sacrifice.

Federal Express was able to put the word *overnight* into the minds of its prospects because it sacrificed its product line and focused on overnight package delivery only.

You don't have to be a linguistic genius to find a winner: Prego went against leader Ragu in the spaghetti sauce market and captured a 16 percent share with an idea borrowed from Heinz. Prego's word is *thicker*.

The most effective words are simple and benefit-oriented. No matter how complicated the product, no matter how complicated the needs of the market, it's always better to focus on one word or benefit rather than two or three or four. Papa John's Pizza used two words, *better ingredients*.

Also, there's the halo effect. If you strongly establish one benefit, the prospect is likely to give you a lot of other benefits too. A "thicker" spaghetti sauce implies quality, nourishing ingredients, value, and so on. A "safer" car implies better design and engineering.

Whether the result of a deliberate program or not, most successful companies (or brands) are the ones that own a word in the mind of the prospect. Here are a few examples:

Crest	Cavities
Mercedes	Engineering
BMW	Driving

Volvo	Safety
Domino's	Home delivery
Pepsi-Cola	Youth
Nordstrom	Service

Words come in different varieties. They can be benefit-related (cavity prevention), service-related (home delivery), audience-related (younger people), or sales-related (preferred brand). But, above all, they must be simple. Which brings me to one of my pet peeves.

COMPLEX LANGUAGE IS CONFUSING

Mark Twain once wrote a letter to a young friend that advised: "I notice that you use plain, simple language, short words, and brief sentences. That is the best way to write English. It is the modern way and the best way. Stick to it."

Alas, more of Mark Twain's thinking is needed in business.

When Shakespeare wrote Hamlet, he had 20,000 words with which to work. When Lincoln scribbled the Gettysburg Address on the back of an envelope, there were about 114,000 words at his disposal. Today there are more than 600,000 words in *Webster's Dictionary*. Tom Clancy appears to have used all of them in his last 1000-page novel.

Language is getting more complicated. As a result, people have to fight off the tendency to try out some of these new and rarely used words.

What if some famous adages had been written with a heavier hand and some fancier words? Here's a sampling of some simple ideas made complex:

- Pulchritude possesses profundity of a merely cutaneous nature. *(Beauty is only skin deep.)*
- It is not efficacious to indoctrinate a superannuated canine with innovative maneuvers. *(You can't teach an old dog new tricks.)*
- Visible vapors that issue from carbonaceous materials are a harbinger of imminent conflagration. *(Where there's smoke, there's fire.)*
- A revolving mass of lithic conglomerates does not accumulate a congery of small green bryophitic plants. *(A rolling stone gathers no moss.)*

You get the point. Good writing and speech can't be confusing. They have to be clear and understandable, and the shorter the better.

BUSINESS HAS
ITS OWN LANGUAGE

If all these new words aren't bad enough, business people are busy inventing their own language. Here is a direct quote from one futurist and management guru: "Managers have come to understand that there are multiple modes of change. One is what I call 'paradigm enhancement,' which the total-quality, continuous-improvement message has been all about. The other is radical change—or paradigm-shift change—which is unlike any other kind of change that you must deal with."

Fortune magazine ("Jargon Watch," February 3, 1997) reported that Better Communications, a firm in Lexington, Massachusetts, that teaches writing skills to employers, clipped these management-speak phrases from what it described as "memos from hell" circulating at Fortune 500 companies.

- Top leadership helicoptered this vision. (*The bosses are looking beyond next week.*)

- Added value is the keystone to exponentially accelerating profit curves. (*Let's grow sales and profits by offering more of what customers want.*)

- We need to dimensionalize this management initiative. (*Let's all make a plan.*)

- We utilized a concert of cross-functional expertise. (*People from different departments talked to each other.*)

- Don't impact employee incentivization programs. (*Don't screw around with people's pay.*)

- Your job, for the time being, has been designated as "retained." (*You're not fired yet.*)

Why do business people talk so mysteriously about things like *core competency* (what we do well) or *empowerment* (delegating) or *paradigms* (how we do things)? It's gotten so bad that in a book titled *Fad Surfing in the Boardroom,* the author, Eileen Shapiro, had to publish a dictionary on nouveau business words, and the *Wall Street Journal* (June 8, 1998) has uncovered a new sport called *buzzword bingo*. Employees tally points in meetings by tracking the jargon and clichés their bosses spout. (*Deliverables, net net,* and *impactfulness* all score points.)

We sense that business people feel that by using these pompous words, they will seem as smart, complicated, and significant as possible. But all it really does is make them unintelligible. All that said, what's a manager to do to fight off complexity? Help is available.

Dr. Rudolf Flesch staged a one-person crusade against pomposity and murkiness in writing. (Among his books is *The Art of Plain Talk*.) He was one of the first to suggest that people in business who write the way they talk will write better.

Flesch's approach would work like this in responding to a letter: "Thanks for your suggestion, Jack. I'll think about it and get back to you as soon as I can." The opposite of his approach would be: "Your suggestion has been received this date, and after due and careful deliberation, we shall report our findings to you."

You have to encourage simple, direct language and ban business buzzwords not only in writing but in talking as well.

SIMPLICITY IN LISTENING

But more than that, you have to encourage simplicity as the way to better listening. Overwhelmed by the incessant babble of the modern world, the skill of listening has fallen on hard times. Studies show that people recall only 20 percent of what they have heard in the past few days.

In a July 10, 1997, article, the *Wall Street Journal* reported that we've become a nation of blabbermouths who aren't listening at all. We're just waiting for our chance to talk.

And if all this weren't bad enough, the newspaper reports, biology also works against attentive listening. Most people speak at a rate of 120 to 150 words a minute, but the human brain can easily process 500 words a minute, leaving plenty of time for mental fidgeting. If a speaker is the least bit complex and confusing, it takes a heroic effort to stay tuned in instead of faking it.

Meetings and presentations that aren't simple and to the point are a waste of time and money. Little will be communicated as people simply dial out. This can be very costly.

A TRUE STORY

Many years ago, an associate and I were leaving a two-hour meeting where a design firm had presented its recommendations in a multi-million-dollar logo design project. As usual, the presenters used terms such as *modality* and *paradigms* and threw in vague references to *color preference*. It was a presentation loaded with obscure and complex concepts. Because of my low rank, I admitted to my fellow worker that I was quite confused by what had been said and asked him for his overview. He suddenly smiled and looked quite relieved. He then went on to admit that he hadn't understood a word that was said but was afraid to admit it so as not to appear stupid.

That company wasted millions of dollars changing a perfectly good logo because no one in the meeting had the courage to ask the presenters to explain their recommendations in simple, understandable language. If they had, they and their logos would have been laughed out of the room.

The moral of this story is that you should never let a confusing word or concept go unchallenged. If you do, some expensive mistakes can be made. Tell presenters to translate their complex terms into simple language. Never be afraid to say "I don't get it." You have to be intolerant of intellectual arrogance.

Don't be suspicious of your first impressions. Your first impressions are often the most accurate.

Don't fight your gut feelings for fear of looking foolish. In some ways the most naïve-sounding questions can turn out to be most profound.

Let's give Peter Drucker, from *The Effective Executive*, the last words on simple language:

> *One of the most degenerative tendencies of the last forty years is the belief that if you are understandable, you are vulgar. When I was growing up, it was taken for granted that economists, physicists, psychologists—leaders in any discipline—would make themselves understood. Einstein spent years with three different collaborators to make his theory of relativity accessible to the layman. Even John Maynard Keynes tried hard to make his economics accessible.*
>
> *But just the other day, I heard a senior scholar seriously reject a younger colleague's work*

*because more than five people could under-
stand what he's doing. Literally.*

SUMMATION
....

**Big strategic ideas
almost always
come in small words.**

Strategy Is
All about Leadership

The role of the CEO is to lead the charge, a point that I make in the last chapter of many of my books.

Strategy, vision, and mission statements are dependent on the simple premise that you must know where you're going. No one can follow you if you don't know where you're headed.

Many years ago, in a book called *The Peter Principle*, authors Laurence Peter and Raymond Hull made this observation:

> *Most hierarchies are nowadays so cumbered with rules and traditions, and so bound in by*

public laws, that even high employees do not have to lead anyone anywhere, in the sense of pointing out the direction and setting the pace. They simply follow precedents, obey regulations, and move at the head of the crowd. Such employees lead only in the sense that the carved wooden figurehead leads the ship.

Perhaps this pessimistic view of leadership skills has led to the explosion of hundreds of books dealing with leadership (most of them being downright silly). There's advice on whom to emulate (Atilla the Hun), what to achieve (inner peace), what to study (failure), what to strive for (charisma), whether to delegate (sometimes), whether to collaborate (maybe), America's secret leaders (women), the personal qualities of leadership (having integrity), how to achieve credibility (be credible), how to be an authentic leader (find the leader within), and the nine natural laws of leadership (don't even ask). In fact, there are 3098 books in print with the word *leader* in the title.

To us, how to be an effective leader isn't worth a whole book. Drucker presents it in a few sentences. "The foundation of effective leadership is thinking through the organization's mission, defining it and establishing it, clearly and visibly. The leader sets the goals, sets the priorities, and sets and maintains the standards."

GO DOWN TO THE FRONT

First, how do you find the proper direction? To become a great strategist, you have to put your mind in the mud of the marketplace. You have to find your inspiration down at the front, in the ebb and flow of the great marketing battles taking place in the mind of the prospect.

The unpretentious Sam Walton traveled to the front lines of every one of his Wal-Mart stores throughout his life. He even spent time in the middle of the night on the loading docks, talking with the crews.

Unlike "Mister Sam," many chief executives tend to lose touch. The bigger the company, the more likely it is that the chief executive has lost touch with the front lines. This might be the single most important factor limiting the growth of a corporation.

All the other factors favor size. Marketing is war, and the first principle of warfare is the principle of force. The larger army, the larger company, has the advantage. But the larger company gives up some of that advantage if it cannot keep itself focused on the marketing battle that takes place in the mind of the customer.

The shootout at General Motors between Roger Smith and Ross Perot illustrated the point. When he was on the GM board, Ross Perot spent his weekends buying cars. He was critical of Roger Smith for not doing the same.

"We've got to nuke the GM system," Perot said. He advocated atom-bombing the heated garages, chauffer-driven limousines, and executive dining rooms.

Chauffeur-driven limousines for the managers of a company trying to sell cars? Top management's disconnection from the marketplace is the biggest problem facing big business.

If you're a busy CEO, how do you gather objective information on what is really happening? How do you get around the propensity of middle managers to tell you what they think you want to hear? How do you get the bad news as well as the good?

If you don't get the bad news directly, bad ideas can flourish instead of being killed. Consider the following parable:

THE PLAN

In the beginning was the Plan.
And then came the Assumptions.
And the Assumptions were without form.
And the Plan was completely without substance.

THE WORKERS

And the darkness was upon the face of the
  workers
as they spake unto their Group Head saying:
"It is a crock of shit and it stinketh."

THE GROUP HEADS

And the Group Heads went unto their Section Heads and sayeth:
"It is a pail of dung and none may abide by the odor thereof."

THE SECTION HEADS

And the Section Heads went unto their Managers and sayeth unto them:
"It is a container of excrement. And it is very strong.
Such that none may abide by it."

THE MANAGERS

And the Managers went unto their Director and sayeth unto him:
"It is a vessel of fertilizer. And none may abide by its strength."

THE DIRECTOR

And the Director went unto the Vice President and sayeth unto him:
"It promoteth growth and is very powerful."

THE VICE PRESIDENT
••••••••••••••••••••••••••••

And the VP went unto the President and sayeth
*   unto him:*
"This powerful new Plan will actively promote
*   the growth*
and efficiency of the Company."

THE POLICY
••••••••••••••••••

And the President looked upon the Plan and
*   saw*
that it was good and the Plan became Policy.

NEEDED: HONEST OPINIONS

One possible way of finding out what's really going on is by "going in disguise" or poking around unannounced. This would be especially useful at the distributor or retailer level. In many ways this is analogous to the king who dresses up as a commoner and mingles with his subjects. The reason: to get honest opinions of what's happening.

Like kings, chief executives rarely get honest opinions from their ministers. There's just too much intrigue going on at the court.

The members of the sales force, if you have one, are a critical element in the equation. The trick is how to get a good, honest evaluation of the competition out of them. The best thing you can do is to praise honest information. Once the word gets around that a CEO prizes honesty and reality, a lot of good information will be forthcoming.

NEEDED: A VISIBLE LEADER

The best leader knows that direction alone is no longer enough. The best leaders are storytellers, cheerleaders, and facilitators. They reinforce their sense of direction or vision with words and action.

There was no greater leader in the airline business than Herb Kelleher, the ex-CEO of Southwest Airlines. He became the king of the low-fare, short-haul airline business. Year after year, his airline has appeared on every list of the "most admired" and "most profitable" companies.

If you've flown Southwest, you've probably recognized the incredible spirit and enthusiasm of the airline's personnel. They even have a sense of humor that, as one passenger put it, "makes flying on that cattle car enjoyable."

Anybody who knows Kelleher realizes that the airline's personality is *his* personality. He is an amazing cheerleader who kept those planes moving and morale high. He was indeed "walking behind them."

119

He also knew his people and his business. In a meeting with Kelleher, I encouraged him to buy one of the East Coast shuttles that were for sale. It would instantly make Southwest a big player in the East.

He thought a minute and said, "I sure would like their gates in New York, Washington, and Boston. But what I don't want is their airplanes and, more importantly, their people."

He sure was right. Cheerleading those East Coast shuttle people would have been impossible.

Kelleher points to another attribute of your best leaders. They tend to live the business and come to personify it. In the heyday of Chase Manhattan Bank, its chairman, David Rockefeller, created news just by visiting foreign heads of state. In effect, he was a head of state.

In his prime, Lee Iacocca personified Chrysler.

Today, Bill Gates personifies Microsoft. He looks like a computer nerd. He sounds like a computer nerd. He lives in a computer nerd's house.

A visible leader is a very powerful weapon for winning customers and prospects. This kind of leader offers unique credentials for a company. (The Germans had a deep respect for George Patton—so much so that the Allies used him as a decoy.)

Also, the troops are proud to follow this kind of leader into battle. They trust such a leader instinctively.

Without trust, there won't be any followers. And without followers, you won't have much of a charge.

IT'S NOT ABOUT THE NUMBERS

If you live by the numbers, you can die by the numbers. CEOs that look at their jobs purely from within the context of pushing the troops to make their forecasts are risking not only their jobs but the health of their organizations. Nothing demonstrates this better than the sad saga of Richard McGinn. He was the CEO of Lucent Technologies and had turned the former equipment-making arm of AT&T into a Wall Street star by increasing sales at a double-digit pace.

But nothing goes up forever, and in 2000 Lucent missed its numbers twice. So the pressure was on the sales troops. From numerous reports in the business press, McGinn's message was to do deals, no holds barred. According to the press, the company promised its customers a host of discounts, one-time credits, and other incentives certain to eat into future sales. When the company badly missed its numbers again, all hell broke loose, and McGinn bit the dust. The stock plunged, and Lucent's future has been put in some doubt. As mentioned earlier, you can die by being too focused on the numbers.

If you get your strategy right, the numbers will follow.

IT'S ABOUT PERCEPTIONS

If there's one lesson to take out of this book, it is this: Successful or failed strategies are all about perceptual problems and opportunities in the marketplace. And it's all about understanding that the mind of the customer is where you win and lose.

You cannot be swayed by those wonderful presentations by your executives on how your company can make a better product or leverage your better distribution or your better sales force to get into the marketplace. You have to stay focused on the mind of the prospect. Minds are difficult if not impossible to change. And if your executives say it can be done, don't believe them. The more you understand the mind of your customer or prospect, the less likely you are to get into trouble.

I once asked one of the ex-CEOs of General Motors if he ever questioned the proliferation of car models that eventually destroyed the meaning of the company's brands (he was a financial person with little background in marketing).

That question caused him to stop and ponder for a few seconds. His response: "No, but I do recall thinking that it was getting a little confusing." His concern was absolutely correct, but he failed to act on his instincts. His assumption was that the executives knew what they were doing. This turned out to be a false assumption. But it took a number of years for this mistake to be felt at GM. Today, thanks to intense competition, mistakes are felt in a matter of months, not years. That's why marketing is too important to turn over to an underling. To survive, a CEO has to assume the final responsibility for what gets taken to the marketplace. After all, your job is on the line.

I once said just that to the head of a very large division of a very large company. While he acknowledged the importance of being involved, he expressed his concern about undercutting the responsibility of those middle-level executives in charge. Well, you have to put those concerns aside if you want to stay out of trouble.

IT'S ABOUT THINKING LONG TERM

Let's just say you've focused on your competitors and figured out their strengths and weaknesses in the prospect's mind. You have searched out the one attribute or differentiating idea that will work in the mental battleground.

Then you have focused all your efforts to develop a coherent strategy to exploit that idea. And you have been willing to make the changes inside the organization to exploit the opportunities on the outside. It's what they call *execution*.

Now you must be willing to take the time to let that strategy develop. Marketing moves take time to develop, so you must—in the face of pressure from Wall Street, the board, and your employees—be willing to stay the course. Nothing demonstrates this better than the example of Lotus Development Corporation, the company that invented the spreadsheet for the PC.

Lotus was overrun by Microsoft's introduction of its own spreadsheet, Excel for Windows. Since Microsoft invented Windows, and Lotus was late to market with a Windows version of its spreadsheet, Lotus was in deep trouble. Jim Manzi, then the CEO, decided to shift the battlefield. To him, the future of the brand had to be *groupware* (software designed for groups or networks of computers, as opposed to software for individual PCs), because Lotus was in the early stages of developing a product called Notes, which became the first successful groupware program. So groupware became the focus as Manzi began the process of building and supporting the Notes and groupware business.

IT'S ABOUT HANGING IN THERE

Getting to where Lotus is today took an enormous effort. When asked about this effort of changing focus, Jim Manzi summed it up as a "brutal process." Here is the story he told me in his own words:

The spreadsheet was the center of gravity at Lotus. It once represented 70 percent of our business. It was our "mainframe" business, so to speak. But Microsoft and Windows really put a big hole in our future.

In the early nineties I felt Notes was the best future we had. Unfortunately, not everyone in the company felt that way. Many wanted to just continue to improve the spreadsheet. During one difficult period, 12 VPs left the company.

They didn't see the future the way I did.

All this, plus the ongoing investment in this product, didn't go unnoticed by our board of directors. Keeping them on the Notes bandwagon required telling the story over and over, maintaining perspective, and building relationships both inside and outside the company.

Once the board loses that vision of the future, your problems magnify.

Luckily the numbers started to get better and people started to get more comfortable with an investment that is closing in on $500 million.

Manzi certainly knew where he was going. The end of the story was a happy one. IBM bought the company for $3.5 billion and has since made Lotus one of the cornerstones of its software efforts with enterprise customers. Lotus was in big trouble, but a bold, long-term effort bailed the company out of a potentially fatal problem.

Manzi's experience is proof that strategy is all about leadership.

LEADERS ARE GOOD GENERALS

Finally, if you're at war, it's important that you adopt the qualities of a good general.

- *You must be flexible.* You must be flexible so as to adjust the strategy to the situation and not vice versa. A good general has built-in biases, but he or she will seriously consider all alternatives and points of view before making a decision.

- *You must have mental courage.* At some point, your open mind has to close and a decision must be made. A good general reaches deep inside to find the strength of will and mental courage to prevail.

- *You must be bold.* When the time is right, you must strike quickly and decisively. Boldness is an especially valuable trait when the tide is running with you. That's when to pour it on. Beware of those who exhibit too much courage when the deck is stacked against them.

- *You must know the facts.* A good general builds strategy from the ground up, starting with the details. When the strategy is developed, it will be simple but powerful.

- *You need to be lucky.* Luck can play a large part in any success, provided you can exploit it. And when your luck runs out, you ought to be prepared to cut your losses quickly. "Capitulation is not a disgrace," said Clausewitz. "A general can no more entertain the idea of fighting to the last man than a good chess player would play an obviously lost game."

Amen to all that.

Despite their expensive suits, fancy automobiles, and corporate jets, do not forget that leaders are ordinary human beings. And because they are human, they can be seduced by power, money, and ego. Wall Street, with its siren song of growth, prestige, and fame, can lead leaders to lose touch with what's really happening in the marketplace and within their organizations.

A PERFECT EXAMPLE

If I were to name one leader as an example, I would pick James D. Sinegal of Costco. His company has been billed as the only company that Wal-Mart fears—and for good reason, because nobody runs warehouse clubs better than Costco. Just look at the numbers. Sam's Club, the Wal-Mart entry, has 70 percent more stores than Costco, yet Costco outsells it ($34.4 billion vs. $32.9 billion). In doing this, the average Costco store generates nearly double the revenue ($112 million vs. $63 million.) How does Sinegal do it?

For one thing, he has a strategy of offering high-end products at deep discount prices. He has captured a breed of urban sophisticates who trade up for exciting products and trade down to private labels of more prosaic products. Wal-Mart merchandises to the mass middle market.

Next, he doesn't let Wall Street run his business. As he put it in a recent *Fortune* article titled "The Only Company Wal-Mart Fears" by John Helyan (November 24, 2003), "I care about the stock price. But we're not going to do something for the sake of one quarter that's going to destroy the fabric of our company and what we stand for."

He has kept himself in the good graces of his subordinates by limiting his pay ($350,000) and not taking a bonus for the past 3 years. He caps his salary and bonus at twice the level of a Costco store manager. (Isn't that refreshing?)

The moral of this story is that the quality of leadership can trump the quantity of resources. As that *Fortune* article reported in a quote from a Costco director and investor, "Here's the difference between Sam's and Costco. We have a live Sam Walton who's still there and Wal-Mart doesn't."

SUMMATION
....
No one will follow if you don't know where you're going.

Strategy Is
All about Reality

In the past decade we've witnessed the troubles and
even failures of some of America's corporate icons.
The likes of Polaroid, AT&T, Xerox, Levi Strauss, Enron,
Lucent, and many others went from hero to bum status.
These were rich companies loaded with talent, sur-
rounded by consultants and courted by Wall Street.
Their leaders were paid millions in annual compensa-
tion and lionized by the media. These companies
became the infamous stars of my book *Big Brands, Big
Trouble*. The strategic lessons they learned the hard way
can be summed up in one simple statement: they all lost
touch with the reality of the marketplace.

THE GROWTH TRAP

In my estimation, Wall Street is at the heart of many strategic mistakes. It often creates an environment that encourages bad, sometimes irrevocable, things to happen. In a way, Wall Street sets up a greenhouse of trouble, and like a greenhouse, what it's all about is encouraging things to *grow*. That desire for growth is at the heart of what can go wrong for many companies. Growth is the by-product of doing things right. But in itself, it is not a worthy goal. In fact, growth is the culprit behind impossible goals.

CEOs pursue growth to ensure their tenure and to increase their take-home pay. Wall Street brokers pursue growth to ensure their reputations and to increase their take-home pay.

But is it all necessary? Not really. When you consider that people do damaging things to force unnecessary growth, you can say that it's a crime against the brand. A true story illustrates how the desire for growth is at the root of evil doings.

I was brought in to evaluate business plans for a large multibrand drug company. In turn, the brand managers stood up and presented their next year's plans. In the course of a presentation, a young executive warned of aggressive new competition in his category that would definitely change the balance of power. But when it came to a sales projection, there was a predicted 15 percent increase. Instantly, I questioned how this could be with the new competition.

His answer was they were going to do some short-term maneuvering and line extension. Long term, wouldn't this hurt the brand? Well, yes. Then why do it? Because his boss made him put in the increase, and I would have to talk with him.

One week later, the boss admitted the problem, but said his own boss needed the increase because of, you guessed it, Wall Street.

THE 15 PERCENT DELUSION

Carol Loomis, a well-known *Fortune* editor, wrote a landmark article (February 5, 2001) on this subject that challenged the "brash predictions about earnings growth that often lead to missed targets, battered stock and creative accounting." The question asked was "Why can't CEOs kick the habit?"

In the article, Loomis laid out what has become accepted executive behavior:

> *Of all the goals articulated, the most common one among good-sized companies is annual growth in earning per share of 15 percent—the*

133

*equivalent, you might say of making the all-
star team. With 15 percent growth, a company
will roughly double its earnings in five years. It
will almost inevitably star in the stock market,
and its CEO will be given, so to speak, ticker-
tape parades.*

You don't have to be a rocket scientist to figure out
why this happens. It's these kinds of predictions that get
Wall Street's attention. It's like a love dance between
Wall Street and management as they whisper sweet
nothings to each other. Management wants the top analysts to follow them and recommend their stock. Wall
Street wants a winner to make analysts look good and
attract more money.

It's all a delusion.

THE REAL NUMBERS

As Loomis points out in her article, extensive research
shows that few companies are able to grow 15 percent or
more a year. *Fortune* looked at the data for 150 companies for three basic time periods over the past 40 years
(1960 to 1980, 1970 to 1990, and 1989 to 1999).

In each of those time frames, only three or four companies achieved the 15 percent or more earnings growth

factor. About 20 to 30 companies ran at a 10 to 15 percent clip, 40 to 60 companies ran at 5 to 10 percent, 20 to 30 at 0 to 5 percent, and 20 to 30 actually ran a negative number. That's right, there were as many big losers as big winners.

Overall, during that 40-year period, aftertax profits grew at an annual rate of just over 8 percent. This means that any company doing 15 percent was running at almost twice the rate of the general population of companies.

With that reality, it's not surprising that companies start to do some bad things to keep their growth rates up.

THOSE IMPOSSIBLE GOALS

Goals are responsible for mucking up marketing plans. I am opposed to them because they introduce unreality into the marketing process.

Managers who are obsessed with what they want to do love to set goals.

What are long-term plans but a meticulous outline of where managers want their company to be in 5 or 10 years? The talk is of market-share and return-on-equity goals.

These types of managers are trying to force things to happen instead of trying to find things to exploit. They tend to chase existing markets instead of looking for new opportunities. They also are internally oriented instead of being externally oriented.

When pressed about goals being nothing but wishful thinking, top managers tend to defend them as being "something to shoot at"—sort of a target. But what these people don't realize is that goal setting tends to communicate an unwillingness to accept failure. Because of this, people will fail to do the right things because they're busy trying to hit those unrealistic goals.

Trying to hit that mythical sales goal will encourage brand managers to push unnecessary line extensions or gin up expensive promotions to load up distribution. But worse, it also keeps them from isolating the problem, facing it squarely, and then going all out to solve it.

Another problem with goal setting is that it creates a certain amount of inflexibility. When you're focused on a goal, you tend to miss opportunities that present themselves when you take a different direction.

IS BIGNESS WORTH IT?

Since we've been discussing all things big and the dangers of growth, it is worth exploring whether that desperate desire to grow is truly worth all the effort.

When you start to study the subject of getting big, you can quickly come up with a stunning amount of research and analysis that seriously questions whether bigger is better. By the time I was finished, I began to wonder what in the world those CEOs were thinking about as they got trapped in the land of mergermania.

When a company is rich and successful, it doesn't want anything to change. IBM didn't want to see its mainframe world shift to small computers. General Motors didn't want to see its big-car world shift to small cars.

As a result, inventions that undercut the company's main business are frowned on. Rare is the big successful company that says, "Hey that's a better idea. Let's dump our original idea." Instead, the managers quickly point out the flaws in this new idea. What they never take into consideration is that this new thing can be improved to a point where it can become what is called a *disruptive technology* or one that shifts the balance of power.

Market leaders have to be willing to attack themselves with a better idea. If they don't, someone else will.

BIGNESS DISGUISED AS CONVERGENCE

One of the current rationales for getting big is that thing called *convergence*. That's where management predicts that technologies are converging, so you have to be in all of them. Nowhere has this song been sung more than in the media world. All six broadcast networks are tied to their film and television production studios, completing the soup-to-nuts integration of the broadcast business. Five companies have jumped into mergermania with both feet (Viacom, Time Warner, Walt Disney, News Corporation, and General Electric).

But, as time rolls on, more and more of these deals have turned out to be problematic. Rather than marketing coups, they have become accounting problems. As Howard Stringer reported in the *New York Times,* "It turns out that these deals are really about purchase accounting for two years, until everybody opens the books and realizes they have been had."

BIGNESS DOESN'T ORGANIZE WELL

Economists do touch on the difficulties of organizing big companies, but to me, the best analysis of managing size comes from British anthropologist Robin Dunbar. In an excellent book titled *The Tipping Point,* Malcolm Gladwell introduces us to Dunbar, whose work revolved around what he called the *social capacity* of humans, or how big a group we can run with and still feel comfortable. Dunbar's observation is that humans gather in the largest social groups of all the primates, because we are the only animals with brains large enough to handle the complexities of that social arrangement. According to Dunbar, the maximum number of individuals with whom we can have a genuinely social relationship, which includes knowing who they are and how they relate to us, seems to be 150.

Gladwell extracted from Dunbar's work the following observation, which gets to the heart of being too big:

> *At a bigger size you have to impose complicated hierarchies and rules and regulations and formal measures to try to command loyalty and cohesion. But below 150, Dunbar argues, it is possible to achieve these same goals informally: "At this size orders can be implemented and unruly behavior controlled on the basis of personal loyalties and direct man-to-man contacts; with larger groups, this becomes impossible."*

PERSONAL AGENDAS

What Dunbar never envisioned was what happens in big companies. All advanced primates have something called a *reflex personal agenda*. It goes like this: when faced with a decision that could be best for the company versus one that could be best for the individual, a large percentage of the time the human primate will opt for the decision that betters his or her career. Another expression for this is *making your mark*.

In all my years in the business, I've never seen a marketing person come into a new assignment, look around, and say, "Things look pretty good. Let's not touch a thing." On the contrary, all red-blooded marketing people want to get in there and start improving things. They want to make their mark. Just sitting there wouldn't feel right. When a company has offices full of people, you've got to expect endless tinkering with a brand. It's how they keep from getting bored.

It's also how brands get in trouble. The more people you have, the more difficult it is to manage them.

CEOs STRUGGLING TO KEEP PACE

All this growth and size has left a number of megacompanies struggling. DaimlerChrysler is cutting 26,000 jobs at Chrysler. Bank of America Corporation and Bank One merged and have had to struggle with high costs.

It's no wonder that the *Wall Street Journal* wrote an excellent article on CEOs struggling with bigness. To the *Journal*, running a company has taken on a "new kind of complexity and a new degree of turmoil." The article summed up the problems neatly:

> *Capital whips around the globe, economics gyrate and consumer tastes turn on a dime. Information travels almost instantly, be it an earning forecast or a nasty rumor. Dumb moves or stumbles are subject to much greater scrutiny. Decisions must be made quickly, with limited information. Vastly expanded over years, operations can make simple everyday functions, like communicating with employees, increasingly difficult.*

It would appear that today's CEO isn't getting much sleep.

KEEPING IN TOUCH

What many CEOs are doing is shifting their energies to the new technologies. One CEO sends periodic e-mails to 30,000 employees asking for feedback. (Help, I'm up to my waist in printouts?) Another has regular video-conferences where he carefully delivers the same speech over and over so as not to send mixed messages. (Help,

I'm being bored to death by the same speech.) And then there's the endless plane travel, whereby a CEO can easily log over 150,000 miles a year. (Help, my body doesn't know what time it is any more!)

But what I really find alarming is the growing need to spend more and more time on public relations and investor relations. One CEO spends a day each week doing this kind of stuff. His reason: "Large investors want access permanently. It has become accepted that you will always talk to major shareholders."

This means someone else has to run the day-to-day business.

Well, there you have it: the CEOs of these big companies haven't got enough time to get involved in some of those important decisions that come back to bite them later. ("I'd like to spend more time on this, but I have to call back a big investor.")

It's no wonder the corporate mortality rate of CEOs is on the rise. They must know their competition and what makes their company unique.

THE REALITY OF THE MARKETPLACE

My advice is that, although CEOs can't keep up with everything today, the one thing on which they can stay focused is the reality of the market. If one of your marketing experts comes to you with a new widget, ask how many widgets like that are already on the market. Then push the marketer to explain why people will buy your widget instead of the others. If there are no good answers, send the marketer back to the drawing board. But, before the marketer leaves, remind him or her that one of the first laws of positioning is "It's better to be first than to be better." That's the reality, not wishful thinking.

The late David Packard, one of the founders of Hewlett-Packard, had a brilliant observation that makes a fitting ending for this book: "Marketing is too important for the marketing department."

SUMMATION
....

Goals are like dreams.
Wake up and face reality.

MORE ON JACK TROUT'S WORK

This book is but a sampler of what has been written on the many aspects of what goes into good strategic thinking. If you want more on a specific subject, the books listed here are where to find it.

MORE ON PERCEPTIONS

Positioning: The Battle for Your Mind

Jack Trout and Al Ries

Published in 1981, this bestselling book has traveled the world, and to many it's the bible on strategy. It also is the most influential advertising book ever written.

Positioning: The Battle for Your Mind
The 20th Anniversary Edition

Jack Trout and Al Ries

Published in 2001, this edition of *Positioning: The Battle for Your Mind* features comments by the authors on what has happened to their predictions over the course of two decades. It's a fascinating retrospective.

The New Positioning
The Latest on the World's
#1 Business Strategy

Jack Trout with Steve Rivkin

Published in 1996, this book updates and adds to the concept of positioning. It includes more psychology, more examples, and the five most important elements in the positioning process. It contains the final words on one of the biggest words in business.

MORE ON COMPETITION

Marketing Warfare

Jack Trout and Al Ries

Published in 1986, this was the first book to lay out how corporations can use military strategy to outmaneuver, outflank, and even ambush their competition. Published in 18 languages, it lays out the most effective competitive model ever developed.

MORE ON TACTICS AND STRATEGY

Bottom-Up Marketing

Jack Trout and Al Ries

Published in 1989, *Bottom-Up Marketing* takes you through the process of building a marketing strategy by starting at the bottom and looking for a tactic to exploit. That tactic is a competitive mental angle. The strategy is a coherent marketing direction that exploits that angle.

MORE ON SIMPLICITY

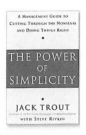

The Power of Simplicity
A Management Guide to Cutting through the Nonsense and Doing Things Right

Jack Trout with Steve Rivkin

Published in 1999, *The Power of Simplicity* is a book about the antidote for complexity in business, common sense. People rely on complexity to mask their ignorance and hedge their bets.

This book presents guidelines for thinking in straightforward terms and cutting through ridiculous jargon. It will help you get your big ideas into small words.

MORE ON THE LAWS

The 22 Immutable Laws of Marketing
Jack Trout and Al Ries

Published in 1993, *The 22 Immutable Laws* lays out the definitive rules that govern the world of marketing. In simple language and with many examples, these laws explain why companies flourish or fail.

MORE ON DIFFERENTIATION

Differentiate or Die
Survival in Our Era of Killer Competition
Jack Trout with Steve Rivkin

Published in 2000, *Differentiate or Die* is an in-depth exploration of today's most successful differentiation strategies. Jack's advice: If you don't have a differentiating idea, you'd better have a very low price. Scott McNealy, CEO of Sun Microsystems, put it this way: "It can make the difference between having lunch or being lunch."

MORE ON REALITY

Big Brands, Big Trouble
Lessons Learned the Hard Way

Jack Trout

Published in 2001, *Big Brands, Big Trouble* is all about learning from mistakes. Written before the recent collapse of the stock market and many of our corporate icons, it explains exactly why it all happened and how to avoid similar events in the future. It's all about how companies fail to live in the real world. It's not what you want to do. It's what your competitors will let you do.

MORE FOR THE CEO

A Genie's Wisdom
A Fable of How a CEO Learned
to Be a Marketing Genius

Jack Trout

Published in 2003, *A Genie's Wisdom* can be considered a CEO's survival guide against inept marketing. With today's CEO under enormous pressure, his or her ability to come up with the right marketing strategy is critical to professional and corporate survival. In this book, a marketing genie coaches a CEO into becoming an expert in pursuing the right strategy. When asked how long it took to write this book, Jack Trout replied, "Forty years."

149

INDEX

About the Author

Jack Trout is president of Trout & Partners, a marketing firm with offices in 13 countries. He has authored or coauthored some of the most important books on marketing, including *Positioning*, *Marketing Warfare*, *Differentiate or Die*, and *The 22 Immutable Laws of Marketing*, which has become "the bible" for marketing professionals. You can reach him at www.troutandpartners.com.